SAND MEW

IGNITE

YOUR

POTENTIAL

The Ultimate Handbook For Visionary Leaders And Business Owners To Take The Brakes Off

Author of International Bestseller

Remember Who You Are

Embody Your Limitless Potential and
Unapologetically Share Your Gifts With The World

First published in 2023 by Sand Mew

© Sand Mew

The moral rights of the author have been asserted.
This book is an Inspirational Book Writers book.

Author: Mew, Sand

Title: IGNITE YOUR POTENTIAL: The Ultimate Handbook for Visionary Leaders and Business Owners to Take the Brakes Off

ISBN: 9798860608146

Editor-in-chief: Rachel Warmath
Cover Design: Sarah Rose Graphic Design

Disclaimer:
The material in this publication is of the nature of general professional advice, but it is not intended to provide specific guidance for particular circumstances, and it should not be relied on as the basis for any decision to take action or not take action on any particular matter which it covers. Readers should obtain individual advice from the author where appropriate, before making any such decision. To the maximum extent permitted by law, the author and publisher disclaim all responsibility and liability to any person, arising directly or indirectly from any person taking or not taking action based on the information in this publication.

DEDICATION

To all of you who are ready to ignite your potential.

"Your playing small does not serve the world.

There is nothing enlightened about shrinking

so that other people will not feel insecure around you.

We are all meant to shine, as children do.

It is not just in some of us; it is in everyone,

and as we let our light shine,

we unconsciously give others permission to do the same.

As we are liberated from our fear, our presence

automatically liberates others."

-Marianne Williamson

"The moment when I realised that I'm the biggest bottleneck in my business, everything changed."

- Yury, Business Owner

WHAT OTHERS HAVE SAID ABOUT WORKING WITH SAND

"**Sand is like talking to 10 experts at once** (...) If you're even thinking about working with Sand, it's a big YES. I can't imagine my life had I not."
— Heidi Cole, Private Flight Attendant +
Confidence In The Air - Coach

"**I've nicknamed Sand 'my Secret Weapon'**"
— Sean Soole, Business Mentor + Educator

"Sand has been remarkable, she is connected, loving, compassionate and holds space so well. **Her difference is that she cares and gets a kick out of seeing others aligning with what is.**"
— Cherri Davis, Founder of OrganiTea Australia

"**Never in my wildest dreams** did I think I could speak so clearly, so powerfully and so in my truth!!"
— Katrina McKechnie, Online Marketer

"**I felt in safe hands, seen, understood and listened to.**
I now feel validated and supported to reach beyond what had previously been my self-imposed beliefs and limitations."
— John Broadbent, Mentor + Author of *Men Unplugged*

"**If I was to explain the essence/ energy of working with Sand** from my experience in one word, it would be: EXPANSIVE."
— Paula Bailey, Leadership Coach

"*Time stands still when you work with Sand.* *If you allow it, magic flows. I wish everyone in the world could go on this journey.*"
— Lauren Bath, Digital Influencer, Director of Lauren Bath Services

"*Sand has very, very clearly done a lot of work on herself* *–you can't get that kind of life experience from a piece of paper.*"
— Georgia Rickhard, Branding Expert;
Editor at Large, Virgin Australia

"*I am blown away at how light I feel, how amazing I feel,* *the hope I have, and the vision I have for what I want to do and how I am going to do it.*"
— Ty Nelson, Athletes Coach

"*Sand is a delightful and insightful presenter.* *She has an amazing amount of knowledge which she shares in an enjoyable and thought-provoking way.*"
— Kevin Blair, General Manager

"*Sand is such a bright light in this world and is so passionate about imparting her knowledge* *- which makes all her trainings a pleasure to be a part of.*"
— Dimity, Blogger

"*I highly recommend Sand Mew and her work.* ***The shifts I've had were crazy.*** *I love the clearing and the healing process and the whole journey. Words can't explain how good it is.*"
— Kamal T., Business Owner

*"**Before working with Sand, I was in a place that had me feeling a bit stuck,** not really sure what was next and how I could achieve my goals.*

*During the process and **since completing The Ultimate Breakthrough Journey / The Group Spiral with Sand yesterday, I feel limitless.***

So much has changed, my mindset, also my reactions in situations. I feel as though no matter what, the universe has my back and I can have the confidence to walk into any situation and know I can have a positive outcome. My purpose feels like it can become a reality (which is huge!). I have a lot more patience, drive and understanding.

As I grow as a spiritually connected human, all relationships around me will organically benefit, the personal relationship will benefit from me being further grounded and determined to complete my goals.

My biggest ah-hahs were that my goals are there to be achieved, no matter how big.

I especially loved the final week, when we did a manifestation clear for my vision of Be, Do, Have across all categories of life.

I can't put the essence/ energy of working with Sand into words. Sand's like nothing I have ever experienced before; a very amazing and unique and spiritually connected human.

If you're thinking about working with Sand, what's stopping you? Jump in and do it right away!"

— Daniel Gaebler, Business Owner +
Author of *The Centred Tradie*

"I have worked with different healers to clear and level myself up but have never had the outcome or results that I've had working with Sand.

She is an amazing healer/coach and I am so grateful that she came across my path in the strange bizarre way that I did. She has helped me to change my life and step into who I am meant to be.

Sand, thank you for sharing your gift and for all the love that you give out to help others bring their light forward!!"
— Sloane Shavel, New York City Reiki Master, Teacher and Practitioner

"Before working with Sand, I was feeling that I was expanding at a rate faster than I was able to deal with and reached out to support this process. (...) The process has helped me to expand and realise my potential is much greater than I had previously believed, based on ingrained beliefs from childhood...

Besides having been able to hit (and bypass!!) several business goals of increasing my mastermind numbers of highly aligned clients and my impact level, I've also been told by my team and clients that I was presenting noticeably more confident and present on stage. I'm also not being as emotionally reactive as I had been. This has shown up in my relationship and with my kids.

Sand is incredibly intuitive and able to read what is going on with accuracy, that at times it's almost unsettling. :)

Her ability to also feel what is going on not only in myself, but my family, her absolute patience, generosity, kindness and zero judgement have been mind-blowing.

I've worked with many other healers/therapists etc before, but Sand has an incredibly rare gift that really makes her stand out.

I found working with Sand was incredibly deep emotionally, though at no point did I feel unsafe to open up and share fully.

Her guidance and patience really help to create one of the calmest, most present environments I've experienced.

The work itself was incredibly powerful and I can see the permanent impact of this every day.

If you are at all thinking about doing the Spiral with Sand, I'd clearly say you have to give it a go. You will feel safe, heard, respected and supported throughout the process. Give it a go, you won't regret it. All I can say is Thank You. :)"

— Sean, Business Mentor + Educator

"Before working with Sand, I was feeling stuck and couldn't move forward in personal or business. It was just like there was a big brick wall in the way.

Through the journey I could feel a change internally but didn't know what it was all about till the 8th week. Then it all came together; the overgrown jungle now had a clear path as such. It all just come together at once. I was blown away by it all really.

I now know the path/ journey that I'm meant to be on. It's all very clear now and I'm working with multiple specialists to get it all into place, which I can do now that my confidence is there to do what's required.

My purpose has completely changed. Now I'm just adjusting everything to work into that. Work's flowing now and I have my drive back to take it where it needs to go.

The journey has also shown me that it's ok to rest and take the time for myself which I'm now fine with doing.

The whole experience was great, but week 8 was definitely the stand out: we did a Manifestation Clear that opened up my next level with such clarity, it was amazing!

Another massive aha moment of my journey was my mission. Absolute wow factor!

Sand is such a calm amazing human with such a great power. *She gives so much to this world. I'm truly blessed to have worked with her.*

I'd describe Sand's essence/ energy as recharging and opening up to step up to the next level.

If you're just thinking about working with Sand, I'd say 100% do it!

Thanks so much Sand for taking me on this journey, it was such an amazing experience!"

— Jake Earl, Visionary Director

TABLE OF CONTENTS

INTRODUCTION

Calling all visionary leaders and business owners! Are you ready to live your wildest dreams? Perhaps you feel ready to hit the next level in your business, but you know something is holding you back. The feeling could be subtle, a knowing inside of you that things could be even better than they already are.

Or perhaps you've hit a major setback, a heavy roadblock, a period where you're sabotaging yourself or you've lost your mojo.

You might feel self doubt, imposter or tall poppy syndrome, overwhelm, anxiety, spinning your wheels, getting triggered or flat.

I have good news!

You're in the right place. I wrote this book for you.

I'm Sand Mew. I'm an igniter. A holistic business mentor, international bestselling author, speaker, entrepreneur and global educator in transformation.

I support visionary leaders, entrepreneurs and business owners just like you to free yourself of lifetimes worth of emotional baggage, conditioning and upper limits, so you can remember who you are, ignite your potential and increase your flow, purpose, wealth and impact.

After more than two decades of study and 20 years of practice, I fuse ancient and contemporary healing practices with modern business strategy, psychosomatics, neuroscience, trauma-release, energetics and aspects of psychology, and apply this expertise within a systematic framework that I underpin with my deep intuition and emotional intelligence.

My approach is highly unique, transformative and enduring.

To some, my work may seem almost magical. My clients have lovingly introduced me as their "Secret Weapon" and "Woo Woo Sand" in the business owner circles.

However, there is a lot of science, many maps and an ancient history behind almost everything I do, which I'll go into some of in this book. The remainder is deep intuition; based on a knowing deep within. This may sound 'magical', however, it's something we can all access within. It's a spark that can get ignited, and, once it burns brightly, will make a huge positive impact on everything you do and everyone else around you. It lives in all of us. And I'll show you how you'll be able to access it within yourself.

The result of this work? Leaders who can finally move forward to achieve their 'big thing' and reach their true potential. Leaders who are ready to become the ideal versions of themselves. Leaders whose dreams were previously unfathomable but are now grounded in reality, firmly within reach and within their hands.

I strongly believe everyone has the power to live their limitless potential and create a life that is equally fulfilling, abundant and impactful.

Each of us has a unique role to play. The more we unlock our potential, the more we can contribute to a positive change in the world. Even if you can't see your role in this yet, it's there, believe me. Seeing visionary leaders, business owners, entrepreneurs, individuals with a calling step into their uniqueness, claim their inner power and ignite their potential makes my heart sing.

It's time to take the brakes off.

You can have it all.

Now, in order to value your energy and time, I'd like to warn you. This book is not for you if you're looking for a quick fix, a pill to swallow or someone else to do the work for you.

It's not for you if you're seeing yourself as a victim of life, that your circumstances are other people's fault and that someone should come and save you.

It's not for you if you're looking for an encyclopaedia of all the things, filled with unpronounceable terminology and peer-reviewed studies from start to finish.

It's also not for you if you strongly believe that you already know everything about yourself and the nature of reality. And that, just because something might be different to what you've heard about before, isn't valid or possible. (Be warned that my approach may challenge a whole lot of what you've come across so far!)

However, if all of the above is not the case, keep reading.

This book *is* for you if you're ready to understand what's really going on when you experience obstacles, self doubt, sabotage and anxiety.

This book is for you if you're ready to overcome feeling anxious, drained, limited by others and triggered, any traumatic and challenging experiences, getting stuck in over-thinking, or if you haven't been getting the results in your business or inner sense of success that you're looking for.

It's also for you if you've been experiencing a period of fast growth and expansion and have a feeling that you can't keep up or are concerned that it may not last.

Or if everything looks and appears to be perfect, but you just can't seem to feel it.

You might simply be yearning for more ease, flow and fulfilment.

You're done with talking things over and over, with avoiding or pretending "it's not that bad", listening to a gazillion audiobooks and podcasts, looking at a million different modalities and mindset strategies (Don't get me wrong, these are pivotal! However, they have a limit of how much they can shift.) You're done with simply pushing on and trying harder, yet still feeling terrible inside.

I'm glad to tell you, there is an easier way. All we need to do is go inwards and ask your body which is a representation of your subconscious.

What you'll find is deep inner certainty, calm and peace, confidence and inner strength. You'll be able to step into your authentic leadership, have improved personal and professional relationships and increased resilience. You'll have clarity, direction and flow, and will be able to manifest the results you desire with ease and inner certainty.

When one of my clients shared his success story and milestones from stage with some of his peers once, he said, *"The moment when I realised that I'm the biggest bottleneck in my business, everything changed."*

What will change for you when you live your true potential and take your life, business, relationships and impact to the next level?

Are you ready?

Let me take you on a journey.

MY STORY

I was five years old when I had my first encounter with my deep inner knowing. I didn't realise at the time what it was, but even then, it was trying to guide me on my life's journey.

My intuition has always been strong, but the seeds of shame and fear are planted early in our lives. I let it drift from my awareness for years, well into my adolescence, until sickness and a near-death experience when I was sixteen ignited my knowing once again.

What began as a journey in self-healing has taken me around the world, diving deep into the wisdom of ancient healers, woven together with natural and modern therapies, psychology, psychosomatics and neuroscience to create a revolutionary framework for healing and mentorship.

After more than two decades of study, many qualifications, 20 years of practice, creating my own accredited modality called *The Footprint Connection*™ (connecting people with their unique footprint on planet earth), facilitating more than 250 *The Ultimate Breakthrough Journeys* (my version of *The Spiral*), tens of thousands of clearings with clients and working with visionary leaders from all over the world for many years, I have synthesised all that I know to offer powerful and transformative experiences to leaders of every kind.

I'm a mother of two beautiful boys. I've run, managed and owned multiple businesses. I'm a serial entrepreneur and investor.

This unique fusion of abilities, skills and experience has not only supported my clients to create more flow, purpose, success, wealth and impact, but also allowed me to build multi 6-figure purpose-led businesses impacting conscious leaders around the globe.

As a practitioner, I help conscious leaders, visionaries and business owners move beyond the limitations they carry consciously and subconsciously, using a systematic approach to overcome their greatest challenges and create the life of their wildest dreams.

I ignite the potential that we all carry within ourselves, providing leaders with greater clarity, alignment and focus, renewed energy and the ability to fully show up and take on what they are meant to bring to this life. Because when we rise in our collective consciousness and share our gifts with the world, we give others permission to do the same, creating ripples of impact for a better world.

Together we rise. The time is now.

THE VARIOUS STAGES OF BUSINESS AND WEALTH CREATION

There are many maps out there that describe the various stages of a business: startup, growth, becoming established, expansion and then exit. There are also many maps that describe the journey of an entrepreneur and wealth creation.

Robert Kiyosaki, the author of the famous book *"Rich Dad, Poor Dad"*, wrote the *"Cashflow Quadrant - Guide to Financial Freedom"*. In this book he dives into the Cashflow Quadrant which consists of the Employee, Self-employed, Business Owner and Investor quadrants which refer to the four main quadrants of society. It explains how people can become wealthy by stationing themselves in one or more of these quadrants. It also shows that the quadrants of the employee and self-employed (i.e. trading time for money) will have a harder time creating time and money freedom (true wealth), than the individual that's progressed into the business owner and/or investor quadrant.

Author Roger Hamilton even goes as far as splitting the wealth creation journey into 9 stages:

1. The 'Infrared - Victim' stage: expenses supersede revenue, characterised by a lot of stress
2. The 'Red – Survivor' stage: the goal is to be cash neutral each month
3. The 'Orange – Worker' stage: money is saved every month, but time is traded for money (at this stage, most individuals feel a lot of relief and have a tendency to get quite comfortable)
4. The 'Yellow – Player' stage: time is no longer traded for money, but there are scalable products on hand
5. The 'Green – Performer' stage: a managing director leads a team who collectively generate revenue, but they still make most of the decisions

6. The 'Blue – Conductor' stage: the individual leads or has set up multiple teams and streams of income and now manages a portfolio of business interests

7-9. The remaining three 'Indigo - Trustee', 'Violet - Composer' and 'Ultra-Violet - Legend' stages: individuals are at the millionaire and billionaire spectrum who are creating or steering ecosystems and economies.

No matter which map or concept we use, each stage and shifting from one stage to another requires different actions and focuses, as the individual shifts from a self-centred approach to a team-centred one, and so forth.

Since 2019 I've been working predominantly with individuals transitioning from the 4. 'Yellow - Player', all the way to the 7. 'Indigo - Trustee' stage, as well as their leadership teams. If we're referring to it from the Cash Quadrant perspective, these individuals have been mostly in the Self-Employed Quadrant, transitioning into the Business Owner Quadrant, and finally into the Investor Quadrant where they are completely financially free.

What I've been finding is that although very specific shifts and focuses are needed at each stage and transition, there is one thing that all of them have in common:

Every new stage in the journey will require a new version of you. There will be different challenges and motivations. Every stage will require you to change your approach; the tactics and strategies that got you to where you are now are most likely not the ones that will get you to your next level. You'll need to let go of old parts of yourself and become the person that you'll be once you have the outcomes you desire.

In other words, you need to **be**come the person that **do**es what's required in order to **have** what you desire or are striving towards. Be, Do, Have is a model for success that emphasizes shifting your identity and changing your actions in order to create the business and life you want.

Ask yourself; What will your future version of yourself be thinking? Would your future you be operating in the same way that you are? Would the decisions you're currently making be the same once you are your future version of yourself?

You need to grow and change. But how do we change?

Coaching, consulting and counselling can all be super powerful; however, when it comes to embodying and becoming a new version and identity of yourself, they can often fall short or take ages. People start feeling like they need to push their head through the wall, go through immense inner pressure or anxiety, feel overwhelmed, or simply avoid progress altogether.

However, it doesn't have to be like that. In order to potently create powerful results, using fast and effective techniques, we need to take the nervous system and subconscious into account. We need to shift beliefs, change patterns and acknowledge and release trauma that's been stored in the body. This in turn will shift our energy and raise our vibration, which in turn can attract a different outcome.

This is where my unique approach comes in.

How This Book is Structured:

You are free to read this book in chronological order, building on the ideas as you go, or you can skip around to the topics that interest you. In saying that, they will all build on top of each other, so sticking to it in order will most likely give you the deepest insights.

I'll provide you with hands-on exercises to try on your own. I'll also include information about the programs and journeys I offer, as well as links to my website where you can find more detail.

At the end of each chapter, there will be key takeaways to support the assimilation of the content.

Let's start with the underpinning concepts first.

PART 1

THE FOUNDATIONS

THE 4 REQUIREMENTS OF CHANGE

In order to create long-lasting change and transformation, and see real results, we need to implement The Four Requisites of Change, adapted from Neuro-Linguistic Programming:

1. **Release:** Let go of what doesn't serve you in order to create space to introduce something new. In this book, I refer to this as letting go of what no longer serves, clearing your baggage and centering.

2. **Set a Goal:** Clearly define what it is that you want to experience instead of continuing to focus on what you don't. In this book, we'll dive into identifying your aligned goals, but also the emotional and overall states you want to be experiencing, in order to create these aligned goals in 3D reality.

3. **Action:** Take aligned and inspired action towards the goal or intention that you have set. This includes keeping on clearing 'stuff' (i.e. obstacles) as they come up. I refer to this as Take The Brakes Off™ which we can powerfully achieve with *The Ultimate Breakthrough Journey (my version of The Spiral)* and *Take The Brakes Off™ - Self Clearing Method*. This leads to 'Active BEing', which means to keep on shifting your inner state, as well as taking inspired action towards your goals. Without aligned action, change (and results) cannot occur.

4. **Focus + Repeat**: Keep focusing on your intention, goal or vision and keep taking action (as in *Take The Brakes Off™ Self Clearing*, shifting your state and inspired action towards your goals).

When combined with Fitts and Posner's 3 Stages of Learning, which will be introduced on the next page, you have the formula for rapid growth and long-lasting transformation.

Most of the information we consume as a society is focused around the "quick fix" that comes from acquiring more knowledge. More and more people are self-publishing books and launching podcasts, but, in my experience, knowledge rarely leads to desired results and outcomes. If it did, everyone consuming knowledge would be "successful". However, you know just as well as I that that's not the case.

Why is this so? Because knowledge alone doesn't create change, nor does it bring results. You need to embody knowledge in order to live it, so it can get reflected in your reality.

According to Fitts & Posner's (1967) three stages of motor learning, there are 3 stages of learning, or transformation: The Cognitive, Associative and Autonomous Stages:

1. Cognitive – Awareness Stage:
When you begin to have an awareness of the challenge or problem to be solved. You do not yet have the knowledge required to solve the problem. It's a mental process only. I.e., You might be experiencing tiredness, brain fog, anxiety, panic or depression, or you might feel full of self-doubt. It's in your awareness so you can do something about it.

2. Associative – Knowledge Stage:
You now have the awareness of the problem and some understanding of how you could go about solving it. You haven't taken any steps towards resolving the problem. I.e., You are learning, and this is what this book is all about. You are taking in the explanations, and are learning, understanding and creating a map on the inside of your being.

3. Autonomous – Transformation Stage:
You have both an awareness of the problem and knowledge, or access to the knowledge to solve the problem. You take action towards solving the problem and experience a transformation as a result. I.e., in the case of you reading this book, in order to really create a transformation with long lasting change, you need to take action and do the clears. Going on the transformational *The Ultimate Breakthrough Journey* and/or learning to self clear with my *Take The Brakes Off™-Method* will be the transformation, because you'll feel the change all the way through your body.

4. Repeat + Embed:

This Stage is an add-on to Fitts & Posner's model. The transformation that we experience in the face of taking action and walking through our challenges leads to the embodiment of the learning. Any learning, once embodied and repeated, leads to permanent change and transformation.

In our case of you reading and learning through this book, I highly recommend doing the exercises that I'm sharing with you. Feel into your body, keep on checking your 'taps' and map the connections in your body. Even better, learn to *Take The Brakes Off™ Self Clearing* or join one of my upcoming journeys. By repeating this over and over, it becomes second nature.

Many years ago, when I came across lots of these tools for the first time myself, I had to go over and over them. I had to remind myself to remember them, and my husband and I literally reminded each other to remember the tools too. After a while they became second nature. I have not thought about those tools for so long, because they've become an innate part of me. I just automatically use them. I automatically readjust my energy internally, regulate my nervous system, reconnect and expand. The same goes for my clients.

It all happens on autopilot, because we've repeated the steps over and over. Therefore, I highly encourage you to take aligned action to let the transformation sink in.

Key Takeaways:

- In order to create long lasting change and transformation, and see real results, we need to implement The Four Requisites of Change: Release - Goal - Action - Focus + Repeat.

- When combined with Fitts and Posner's 3 Stages of Learning: the Cognitive, Associative and Autonomous stages; and the added Stage of 'Repeat + Embed', you have the formula for rapid growth and long lasting transformation.

HOW YOU CREATE YOUR REALITY

I like to refer to the analogy of an iceberg. The tip of the iceberg that's sticking out of the black waters is representing your conscious mind. It encompasses all that you are currently aware of. This includes memories, thoughts and your awareness around what you like and don't like, things that trigger you, etc.

The body underneath the black waters represents your sub-or unconscious mind. No one knows the shape or size of it, nor what it holds. It encompasses your 'Shadow;' anything you say, think, believe or display that you are currently not aware of.

Approximately 95% of your reality is created by your subconscious mind. That means that your conscious mind only creates about 5% of your reality! Let that sink in.

So, what is your subconscious mind made of?

Approximately 40% of it is governed by collective baggage from about 40 generations that came before us. This takes us back to the 5th and 6th centuries! We don't need a degree in history to understand that there have been a lot of wars, persecutions and trauma that have occurred, especially when it comes to sharing new or different ideas. Therefore, there is a collective fear of speaking up and showing up authentically in our truth. It's been literally historically proven to us that it's not safe to do so.

All of this is stored in our subconscious, influencing us unknowingly every single day and holding us back from living from an empowered and embodied place. Add to this your own past life experiences, ancestral baggage, this life's experiences, lessons and traumas. All of which have formed your beliefs, filters, patterns and conditioning. You can see, there is a lot playing into this.

Therefore, when you have a goal you want to achieve (in your conscious awareness) that your subconscious may deem threatening or scary, guess what will happen?

That's right. It won't.

Only about 5% of your reality gets created by your conscious mind. Most likely you're aware how powerful your mind is. We can create amazing things from sheer willpower alone. However, if we think that we are living our potential doing so, we're far from it. Using your mindset and shifting it is key, I fully agree. However, when we only focus on our conscious mind alone, we limit ourselves to about 5% of our potential.

If we want things to be easier, have less resistance and create change without having to work so hard, we need to unlock our potential via the subconscious; the unconscious part of our being which creates about 95% of our reality.

So how do we access the subconscious?

Through our bodies.

Key Takeaways:

- Approximately 95% of our reality is created by our subconscious mind, of which approximately 40% are governed by collective baggage from about 40 generations that came before us.

- All of this is stored in our subconscious, represented by the body, influencing us unknowingly every single day and holding us back from living from an empowered and embodied place.

- If we want to change our reality, we need to access our subconscious.

YOUR BODY IS A REPRESENTATION FOR YOUR SUBCONSCIOUS

A huge percentage of all the physical experiences that we have, including conditions and illnesses and diseases are from underlying emotional patterns, beliefs and trapped emotions that are stored in our body and have gone unnoticed. Dr. Bruce Lipton, a highly renowned and respected cell biologist, released a Stanford University Medical School research in 1998, in which he stated that stress is the cause of at least 95% of all illness and disease.

According to traditional Chinese medicine, which is more than 3000 years old, health means that all our body parts and organs can fluently communicate with each other as one large organism. In that case, we experience ease and flow. When there is some form of disease, or dis-ease, there is a blockage or miscommunication between two or more body parts, that makes us feel unwell. Very much like in a company, in which every role needs to be filled and communicate effectively with each other, or an automation in which each step needs to effectively trigger the next, the body requires the same.

If one of the team members is down, not working optimally or striving for a different agenda, this will lead to the company not operating optimally, all the way to the overall mission of the company to falter or change direction. Therefore, when it comes to managing the company, there will be KPIs, team meetings and performance management strategies to keep everyone and everything working optimally.

The same goes for your body, according to Traditional Chinese Medicine. The aim is to remove any blockages and balance any excess energies or deficiencies in all areas, so all body parts, organs and cells can return to a state of homeostasis, in which they can communicate fluently with each other.

Your body is a representation for your subconscious. It holds onto all sorts of memories, beliefs and perceptions for you - a ton of messages. These messages might show up in the form of niggling feelings, dreams or passing thoughts, or get stored in the body in the form of tension, blockages, constrictions, flattering sensations and emotions.

You might wonder, what are these messages actually for?

They are here to guide you home to your centre and to help you remember who you are. Every single one of your body's messages better enables you to understand yourself and who you are.

Your body will only let these messages go, if you are willing to stop and acknowledge and then release them. If you don't listen, their volume gets turned up, so you can't ignore them any longer. As a result, these niggling feelings turn into a bigger thing. They want to be heard, acknowledged and seen. Therefore, they send a stronger, more visible message for you to understand, as in disease, illness, chronic ailments or injuries.

You might have an accident and hurt your knee, or run your shin against the table, break your leg, shoulder or elbow, or you get an earache. It totally depends on the holistic picture of what's going on within you; your thoughts, perceptions, feelings and experiences, and of course what accidents or what conditions and illnesses are occurring that give us a precise insight into what is truly going on for you underneath the surface. This holistic picture will then also give us a clear understanding of who you are, what your gifts and message is, as well as your most aligned pathway of what exactly needs to be prioritised, shifted and worked on to get you closer to your Limitless Potential and experiencing wellbeing, health, love and abundance on all levels.

The more you learn to listen within and learn to read those signs, the more you can help yourself and the more easily your subconscious can speak to you. In other words, the more we get to know ourselves and the language of our body, the more we empower ourselves to become the creator of our reality.

Otherwise, our body has to hold onto all those things for us that we haven't fully acknowledged, healed or released yet, and therefore will hold us back.

The more you want to unlock your potential, the more you want to free yourself of those patterns that are holding you back.

The easiest pathway to do so is through the body. Listen to those sensations you're having; no matter if you've got a lump in your throat, a tension in the chest, niggles or pains, they all speak to you. You might not be able to understand their language yet, as there is an art to this listening.

Your body has its own language that takes time and energy to learn. However, it's not rocket science, and you can always get support from someone who is well versed in its language and can act as a translator.

But if your body speaks to you, please understand that there is a message in every little thing you feel. And the more you uncover the underlying reasons and root causes, the more you can be free of the sensations, wiser for their messages and unlock your true potential.

The more you listen and get to understand yourself, the more your subconscious becomes conscious, and the more clarity you'll discover around your ever-expanding purpose and your next steps. Furthermore, this is a felt sense of understanding, true embodiment of the lesson, not just an understanding on a cognitive level.

The result is inner certainty and a deep sense of knowing who you are.

A big part of my journey was overcoming sickness first and experiencing the total disconnection of my body, mind and spirit when I was 16. I actually just needed to return to myself and learn to really listen closely to my intuition. I didn't hear and I didn't listen to that message for quite a few years in my teenage years. I partied, drank and got overly busy. Moreover, I felt torn and pulled into the stuff of my loved ones. I didn't take the time and space to turn within. So it was inevitable that the day had to come when my body said, "No more," and got very ill.

This experience got me into natural therapies, got me to truly 'land' the concept that our body, mind and spirit (or higher consciousness) are all connected and reflecting each other at all times (when we chose to listen) and that stress is a killer, if we let it dictate our lives.

I've also suffered from migraines and headaches for the first 22 years of my life. They were debilitating. Apart from first going the traditional route, then getting chiropractic alignments, working with a naturopath, TCM practitioners, bodyworkers and later on changing my diet, I had to dig really deep and unearth some really deep stuff that went even back into my ancestral line. Once resolved, the headaches and migraines stopped immediately and haven't come back since.

I did not expect this at the time. However, both of these experiences were one of the main reasons why I learnt and embodied that there is way more to everything that we experience than what appears logical to the mind and eye.

This awakening, where we are getting forced to listen, happens to many of us at some point in our lives. Often it is the reason that takes us to natural therapies, a more conscious and awake approach, or simply wanting to help others. We get sick, or get shaken up in some other profound way, and are forced to finally stop and look at everything we do.

If this has been or is you, you'll most likely have found that conventional forms of treating it or dealing with the presenting issue won't help. You might even find that there are several health conditions, injuries or patterns popping up in your life. These are often misleading you in all sorts of directions, while you are trying to find a cure or way out of their pain. I've been finding, however, that if we look at these problems holistically and assess their root cause, they will all come together to form one congruent picture.

What I find is that when we look at the whole picture of all experiences, struggles, health conditions and injuries, and into what they represent and are associated with somatically, we can really tell so much more about who a person is. It tells us where they're coming from and where they're supposed to go to find their fullest expression, which in turn leads to happiness, fulfilment and abundance.

How accustomed you've been to listening to your body up to this point will determine just how much insight you can gain into where your path is leading and what it is best supported with.

I invite you to look deeper, learn the language of your body and go all in. You have all the answers locked into your body. The answers are all here, you just need to learn the language to understand them or get support from a professional who'll be able to translate the messages for you.

In the end, it's often those things that we fear and avoid the most that are actually shifted the quickest, and that are actually holding the most kind, warm and loving messages ever.

If you're ready to understand and dive deeper, read my first bestseller *Remember Who You Are* or learn *Take The Brakes Off™ Self Clearing*. I am sharing some of the somatics, and in the course you'll learn how to test with kinesiology so you can get answers straight from your subconscious (without the ego getting in the way). I'll teach you how to really listen to your body in order for you to unlock more of your potential — quickly and potently.

Key Takeaways:

- Stress is the cause of at least 95% of all illness and disease.

- According to traditional Chinese medicine, health means that all our body parts and organs can fluently communicate with each other as one large organism. The goal is to remove any blockages that interrupt this communication.

- Our body is a representation for our subconscious, holding onto all sorts of memories, beliefs and perceptions for us-a ton of messages. The more you listen and get to understand yourself, the more your subconscious becomes conscious, and the more clarity you'll discover around your ever-expanding purpose and your next steps.

THE NERVOUS SYSTEM

Now let's look at the nervous system. The nervous system transmits signals between the brain and the rest of the body, including internal organs. In this way, the nervous system's activity controls the ability to move, breathe, see, think, and feel our environment.

There is a reason why you can't outthink the body and how you feel. (Have you ever tried telling yourself to be happy when you feel terrible? Or to simply relax when you're feeling completely overwhelmed or tense? And did it work?)

It all goes back to a dysregulated nervous system and afferent nerves. 80% of the nervous system is afferent, which means running from the body towards the brain. This means that only 20% of our nerves run down from the brain to the body. Physical bodily input talks to this 80%, and mindset to the other 20%.

So what is a dysregulated nervous system?

Let's start with looking at stress.

I mentioned that 95% of all illnesses go back to stress. But what is stress? Why do we experience it and what actually happens in the body as a result of it?

We experience stress as an internal response to external challenges and changes. These can be just as much mental as they can be tangible factors; i.e. a lost key, relationship issues, deadlines at work, putting yourself under pressure, running late for an important appointment, chemical or environmental stressors, you name it. Of course, it could also just be our imagination running wild when lacking sleep.

Our stress response is a signal that our body and all its major systems have been activated. This classic fight-or-flight reaction is not just in our heads. It's an automatic response that reverberates throughout our entire body. Adrenaline is released, muscles tense up, our stomach tightens, our heart rate quickens, breathing becomes shallower, blood vessels on the skin surface contract, blood pressure rises, and digestion and intestinal processes shut down.

None of these conditions are meant to persist for very long. They are short-term responses to immediate perceived dangers. However, if we are constantly under stress, our body learns to stay in this state of high alert, which leads to nervous system dysregulation.

In the 90s, Dr. Stephen Porges developed the Polyvagal Theory. It proposes that the autonomic nervous system ("ANS"), and the 3 main physical states it shifts between, are largely responsible for our adaptive behavioural strategies. Those three distinct neural circuits are:

- The Ventral Vagal Circuit (rest and digest)
- The Sympathetic Circuit (fight or flight)
- The Dorsal Vagal Circuit (freeze or shutdown)

Each of these circuits is responsible for different aspects of the body's response to stress and danger.

Our nervous system has a so-called "window of tolerance". This refers to how much stress it can tolerate before it shifts into one of the two survival responses: the heightened stress response (The Sympathetic Circuit) or a shutdown response (The Dorsal Vagal Circuit).

We live in a society that is constantly presenting us with stressful situations. Some are very specific, such as challenges at work, financial pressures, and family issues. Others are rather vague, generalised feelings of being at the mercy of others and forces beyond our control. No matter what, they can feel extreme to our body and nervous system, depending on our levels of resilience.

If this extreme stress load persists, the body will be showing signs of exhaustion, eventually leading to burnout, a condition in which the body is unable to cope with further stress due to mental, emotional and / or physical exhaustion. No wonder that, after what's happened in the world since 2020, burnout rates are sky-rocketing and anxiety is at an all-time high. Depending on which sources you look into, currently about 30% of Australians have some level of anxiety and in the United States, Boston College researchers found reports of anxiety increased to 50 percent and depression to 44 percent by November 2020 — rates six times higher than 2019[1]!

This is despite the rise of the wellness and personal development industry and the huge amount of information available at our fingertips these days. And I believe that all information in the world won't change these statistics unless we start focusing on the body (as representation of the subconscious) and the nervous system and start clearing and self regulating.

Key Takeaways:

- 80% of the nervous system is afferent, which means running from the body towards the brain, which is the reason why we can't outthink the body, when feeling stressed or triggered.

- Our nervous system has a so-called "window of tolerance". It refers to how much stress it can tolerate before it shifts into one of the two survival responses: the heightened stress response (The Sympathetic Circuit) or a shutdown response (The Dorsal Vagal Circuit).

- It's not surprising that, after what's happened in the world since 2020, burnout rates are sky-rocketing and anxiety is at an all-time high.

---

[1] Retraction to: Trends in mental health symptoms, service use, and unmet need for services among U.S. adults through the first 9 months of the COVID-19 pandemic, *Translational Behavioral Medicine*, Volume 12, Issue 7, July 2022, Page 782, https://doi.org/10.1093/tbm/ibac010

ALLOSTATIC LOAD

Generally, people are led to believe that stress, anxiety and burnout are simply MENTAL health conditions. In the short term, this is often the case. However, when it comes to chronic stress, there are many second order effects that are not immediately apparent. When stress is transient and more acute, it simply passes most of us by. Our bodies and nervous systems naturally regulate back to their resting stress baselines. However, when stress becomes chronic, the body can't resolve it and stores the unprocessed stress as so-called "allostatic load" in the body and nervous system.

We consciously or unconsciously feel that we can't cope or aren't good enough. We lose faith in our ability to adequately respond to specific situations, people, or the world at large.

Depending on how much allostatic load is being built up, chronic stress leads to a dysregulated nervous system, as the nervous system holds onto more and more of it and therefore becomes less flexible. This causes many changes on a physiological level and affects the following:

- Processing of stress / resilience
- Mood and emotions
- Creativity
- Ability to focus and perform
- Digestion and the gut
- Sleep quantity and quality
- The immune system
- Ability to socialise

Nervous system dysregulation is a condition in which the body's stress response becomes constantly activated, even in the absence of a stressful situation and long after a stressful or perceived threat has passed. It becomes more prone to moving into fight, flight or shutdown responses and can lead to immediate effects on our mental clarity, emotional wellbeing and performance, if not managed properly. (If you're finding that you're more reactive and easily triggered than in the past, this would be why.)

With high allostatic load, the nervous system shifts into a dysregulated state more easily, making it more difficult to remain in the play state where our performance is at its best. It's also more difficult to shift into the Stillness state in order to wind down each night.

Apart from subconsciously trying to distract us from what is actually going on deeply beneath the surface, excessive adrenaline stimulation unfortunately depletes vital vitamin and mineral stores from our bodies. These include those that are essential for our immune system like Vitamin C and B.

It can also cause a build-up of fatty substances on the walls of our blood vessels and damage the functioning of our digestive systems. Increased cortisol levels lead to an increased storage of adipose tissue, in other words: fat cells, causing some chronically stressed people to gain lots of weight. Often this increase is also some form of subconscious (energetic) protection.

Also, a long-term rush of adrenaline causes our body's kidney energy to deplete. In traditional Chinese medicine, the kidneys are the holders and restorers of our body's own energy, called Chi or Ki. If our kidneys get exhausted due to adrenaline overload, we end up with conditions such as adrenal burnout or chronic fatigue.

Under chronic stress, people are prone to more frequent and more severe viral infections, such as the flu or common cold. Simply put, stress breaks down our body's natural defence, our immune system, as well as negatively influencing some of our major bodily functions. Relaxation, or better: regulation, on the other hand, strengthens them.

The following signs and symptoms suggest a dysregulated nervous system, although there are many ways in which dysregulation can manifest in our personal lives:

- Edginess, irritability and the inability to relax
- Emotional volatility including crying spells for no apparent reason
- Hypervigilance
- Chronic anxiety or depression
- Chronic stress
- Chronic tiredness or fatigue
- Insomnia
- Chronic pain
- Unresolved aches & pains
- Fibromyalgia
- Digestive issues like heartburn, IBS, bloating, indigestion or diarrhoea
- A compromised Immune system and frequent infections
- Brain fog or trouble concentrating

According to Dr. Joe Dispenza, humans are addicted to chemicals within our body. These are either stress related ones, such as cortisol, or happy ones like endorphins.

Considering the Scale of Consciousness by Dr Hawkins which ranges from 0-1000 (see image), and the fact that more than 85% of humanity are resonating at a level of consciousness below 200, a consciousness characterised by fear and survival mode as opposed to thriving, we can see just how many people are dependent on the adrenaline rush of stress! They need more and more of it, to satisfy their addiction to the chemicals in their body that keep pumping them through their day. Therefore, it comes as no surprise that people keep creating situations in their lives to keep them in this all too familiar stress mode. It keeps the adrenaline flowing.

This explains why some people can't seem to ever switch off. They find that they can't relax, even if they have nothing to worry about. Their mind wanders relentlessly and keeps busy until it finds something else to worry, fear or stress about - even if this something lies in the future. Then, once it has found something, it eases off, as it's now back in the familiar state of high stress again. This way it keeps perpetuating itself.

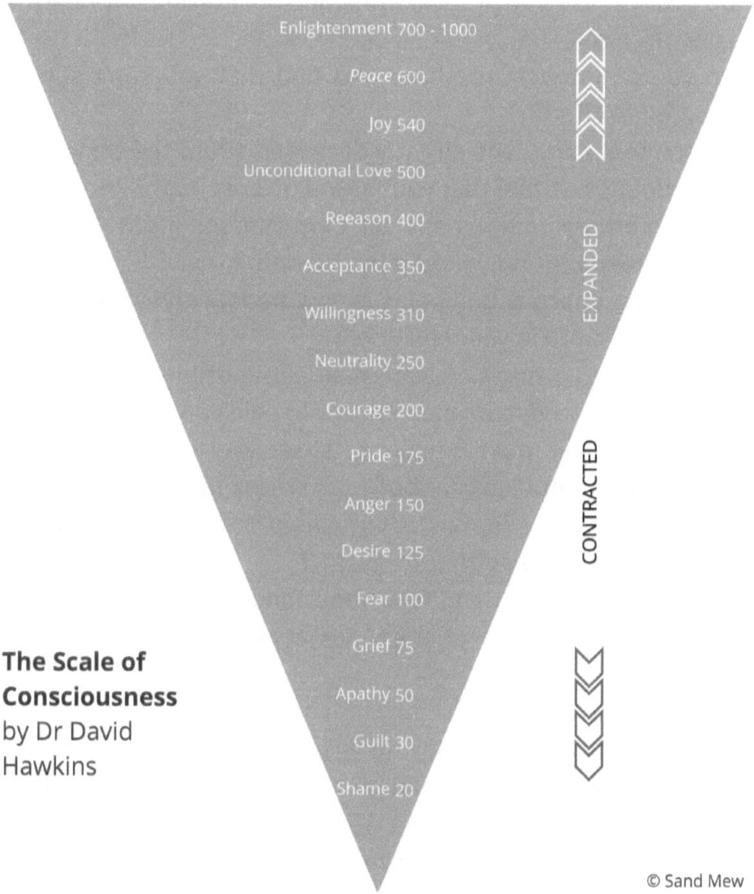

The Scale of
Consciousness
by Dr David
Hawkins

Enlightenment 700 - 1000
Peace 600
Joy 540
Unconditional Love 500
Reeason 400
Acceptance 350
Willingness 310
Neutrality 250
Courage 200
Pride 175
Anger 150
Desire 125
Fear 100
Grief 75
Apathy 50
Guilt 30
Shame 20

EXPANDED

CONTRACTED

© Sand Mew

To make it easier to pinpoint when a dysregulated nervous system is present and burnout is slowly creeping its way into your life, I've put together a checklist of 15 questions to ask yourself. You'll be able to use this list whenever you're going through a busy phase of your life and keep yourself in check that way:

1) Do you get grumpy and short with people easily?
2) Do you fly off the handle at the drop of a hat?
3) Do you get frustrated easily?

4) Do you feel like you're stagnating and not getting anywhere with all your efforts?

5) Do you feel constantly tired and find that you can't seem to get yourself excited?

6) Do you feel bored and slightly detached about the things you need to be doing, but feel that you're kind of 'over it all'?

7) Are you procrastinating and can't get yourself motivated?

8) Do you keep hurting yourself by accident?

9) Do you get sharp or dull pains in your middle and lower back, which used to be more in your shoulders?

10) Do you keep getting sick, have headaches or feel yourself generally getting more and more susceptible to colds and flus?

11) Do you get less than 8 hours of sleep every night in which to re-charge and revitalise your body...or are we talking way less?

12) Do you struggle falling or staying asleep, no matter how tired you are?

13) Do you find you're getting forgetful?

14) Do you lack the ability to focus and concentrate on your tasks?

15) Do you feel anxious a lot or get anxiety attacks?

If you've been finding yourself saying yes to most of these questions, you might realise that all of this exhaustion and your mood swings haven't just been a side effect of working hard, running a business and/or having a family. You might actually have a large allostatic load, be burning out and / or have a dysregulated nervous system!

The reason why millions of people are currently struggling is because they not only have to cope with their current stressors such as financial pressures, uncertainty, wars etc. They also have to deal with the accumulated allostatic load from the last few years. Considering that most nervous systems haven't been trained to adequately discharge and 'clear' their stress load and come back to centre and a regulated state, it's no wonder that most people's window of tolerance has gotten so much smaller.

Many MENTAL health solutions have fallen short, because, just like the name suggests, they focus on the mind and therefore don't address the allostatic load that has accumulated.

In a nutshell; we need to focus on the overall relationship of our mind, body and energy.

With nervous system regulation and clearing, we seek to not only reverse this process, by reducing the buildup of allostatic load, but also strengthen the nervous system and your connection with your body and potential.

There are many ways to relax our bodies; for example, doing sports, dancing, yoga, meditation etc. However, one of the most powerful ways to relax and regulate, whilst simultaneously activating a normalisation of body functions, is reflexology.

Reflexology is a proven method to help you deeply relax and let go of stress from your body. It's based on the principle that certain parts of the body, such as the feet, hands and ears, reflect the whole body. By effective stimulation of these reflexes, the body starts progressively clearing blockages, re-establishing energy flows and balancing itself, resulting in better health.

It's easy to learn the basics of reflexology, and the profound relaxation you experience through it improves circulation, assists in the release of toxins, harmonises and normalises body functions as well as increases energy and wellbeing. Additionally, if combined with the right skills and knowledge (Note: this is not referring to the usually very basic skills of a therapist at the corner spa!), it can enable your body to release trapped emotions, patterns and beliefs which is pivotal when it comes to dealing with the root cause and unlocking our true potential and purpose. We'll be going into these concepts within the following chapters.

For a list of fast, free and super effective tools and techniques which are easy to use and can be incorporated into anyone's busy schedule, feel free to refer to the resources at www.TheFootprintConnection.com. You'll find tips, blog posts and downloadables with Reflexology tips to directly support your nervous system.

When you simultaneously learn to clear, centre yourself, realign your nervous system and develop nervous system resilience, brain fog lifts, stress and anxiety disappears, energy returns, you feel more calm and able to cope with what life presents you and so much more. The effects of *Take*

The Brakes Off™ Self Clearing, however also basic forms of nervous system regulation, are generally experienced as profoundly transformative.

If you'd rather not learn to do any body work, but would like to empower yourself with the extremely potent tool of *Take The Brakes Off™ Self Clearing* for your life and business, or be guided and supported on a deeply transformative journey to clear the largest amount of emotional baggage, allostatic load, conditioning and upper limits within the shortest amount of time, please refer to www.sandmew.com.

If you are noticing that you get stressed and triggered easily (i.e., get anxious, snappy, shut-down or angry), please make use of any and all of these tools often.

They won't just drastically reduce your stress levels and reconnect you with yourself. They will also enable you to tell your intuition apart from your conditioning. In other words, you'll be able to differentiate between 'the shoulds' and 'the musts' versus your own knowing with much more ease and certainty. They will help you to nourish your body, mind and spirit at the same time and leave you with a big sense of empowerment, clarity and confidence.

Therefore, it's vitally important to make sure you help your body return to optimum health and a regulated nervous system on an ongoing basis by releasing stress, whether it's physical, mental, emotional or energetic. It's just as important as listening to your intuition and to your body, in order to tap into your limitless potential.

Key Takeaways:

- When stress becomes chronic, the body can't resolve it and stores the unprocessed stress as so-called "allostatic load" in the body and nervous system. This in turn leads to a decrease in our "Window of Tolerance".

- With high allostatic load, the nervous system shifts into a dysregulated state more easily, which is a condition in which the body's stress response becomes constantly activated, even in the absence of a stressful situation and long after a stressful or perceived threat has passed.

- Many MENTAL health solutions have fallen short, because, just like the name suggests, they focus on the mind and therefore don't address the allostatic load that has accumulated. In a nutshell; we need to focus on the overall relationship of our mind, body and energy.

TRAPPED EMOTIONS

We all have emotions. We are emotional beings and our emotions are experienced in response to our environment. Emotions are energy in motion and are a normal part of life, as we experience and interpret the world through them. In traditional Chinese medicine, we have 5 elements for all of the 14 meridians. 12 of them are linked to organs that represent a main emotion. For example, the liver corresponds to the emotion of anger and the lungs to the emotions of sadness and grief. In order to lead a healthy, full life, we need to move through all emotions fluently. Emotions are supposed to be felt, processed by the body, mind, and spirit connection, and then at some point let go of. This is usually the trajectory of positive emotions which result in you feeling good.

On the other hand, in society we've learnt that some emotions are apparently not "as good" as other ones, and those not so favourable emotions often follow a different trajectory. For example, people tend to strive to be happy and joyous, and suppress emotions such as anger, frustration or sadness. It's not that these emotions aren't there and part of their lives; they are just not as welcome and therefore not allowed to be expressed. Just think of all those times that parents tell their kids, *"Shhh don't cry"*. We hear from a young age that crying, feeling sad or frustrated aren't acceptable and are bad emotions. So we end up suppressing them instead.

Also, emotions resulting from pain or distress can be so strong that they can't get processed completely. This can happen in many situations. For example, if we got told off in class in front of everybody else and felt small and stupid for it, or if we went through bigger things like a car accident, abuse or family split-ups the resulting emotions may be so strong and big we can't process them. It doesn't matter if it's a big or tiny event, if we feel strongly about something, we usually make a decision of some kind in response to it. For example, *"I'll never do xyz again!"*, *"I'll never let this happen to me again!"* or *"I hate...!"*

When this happens, some remnant of the negative emotional energy becomes trapped in the body, usually in an organ or gland, although it can become trapped anywhere in the body or in the field of energy surrounding the body. Remember, no matter what the reason or catalyst for the emotion, it's never really as much about what happens as it is about what the person on the receiving end perceives.

For example, three people can go through exactly the same situation, but all three of them can experience the situation in COMPLETELY different ways. One might flow through it, release it and never think of it again, the other person might dwell on it for the rest of their life, and the third person might find it so traumatic that they ban the experience from their memory altogether. The third way would still affect this person subconsciously—until the day comes that he/she chooses to work on acknowledging and releasing their subconscious blockages.

The reason why the trapped emotion would affect the person (sub) consciously is that the frequency (rate of vibration) of a trapped emotion is different from the frequency of the body part in which it is trapped. This conflicting frequency begins to distort the normal, healthy frequency of that body part. At some point in time, this distortion or imbalance of the tissues or energy field will cause symptoms such as uneasiness, emotional ups and downs, depression, and/or physical symptoms. However, most of the time we have no idea that what is causing these symptoms are trapped emotions.

As a result, we respond differently to situations than someone else who doesn't have the same trapped emotions and beliefs. This leads to our whole body showing signs such as hanging shoulders, a hunched back or misaligned spine, and symptoms associated with the organ or body part in which the emotion is trapped.

If not released, trapped emotions cause imbalances that encumber us and block us from going for our dreams, believing in ourselves and leading full lives. They can affect us physically and literally make us sick, just as much as they can affect us mentally and emotionally. The good news is that trapped emotions can be released via various forms of healing; i.e. self-clearing, trauma release techniques, dancing, certain types of bodywork, breathwork, and the feet with *The Footprint Connection Reflexology*™, to name a few. You can take your life back, ditch sabotage, go for your dreams, enjoy better health and experience more fulfilment.

You're born for amazing things — don't let your trapped emotions hold you back!

Key Takeaways:

- Emotions are energy in motion and are a normal part of life, as we experience and interpret the world through them. If we don't express, but suppress or can't process them fully, they end up getting trapped.

- The reason why the trapped emotion would affect the person (sub) consciously is that the frequency (rate of vibration) of a trapped emotion is different from the frequency of the body part in which it is trapped.

- If not released, trapped emotions cause imbalances that encumber us and block us from going for our dreams, believing in ourselves and leading full lives.

BELIEFS AND HOW
THEY CREATE OUR REALITY

Let's talk about beliefs and how they create our reality, including mirror theory.

We create our reality either on a conscious, but most often a subconscious, level. Our conscious mind only perceives a fraction of what our subconscious mind does. Our brain processes 400 billion calculations per second, of which only 40 billion get processed via the conscious mind. Compare this to a computer which usually can only calculate 100 billion calculations a second!

Information comes in on a conscious level. You then make decisions and take actions based on your neuro-associations, meta programs, beliefs and values. Our conscious mind doesn't let ourselves receive all the information around us, because it would be too much. So it filters it.

Therefore, literally anything we experience is simply a mirror of our internal environment. This doesn't mean that it doesn't exist outside of us, no. However, we will never really experience an unfiltered, unbiased, unconditioned view of it. So there's never really 'the truth' or one truth. There is only our truth.

NLP Communication Model

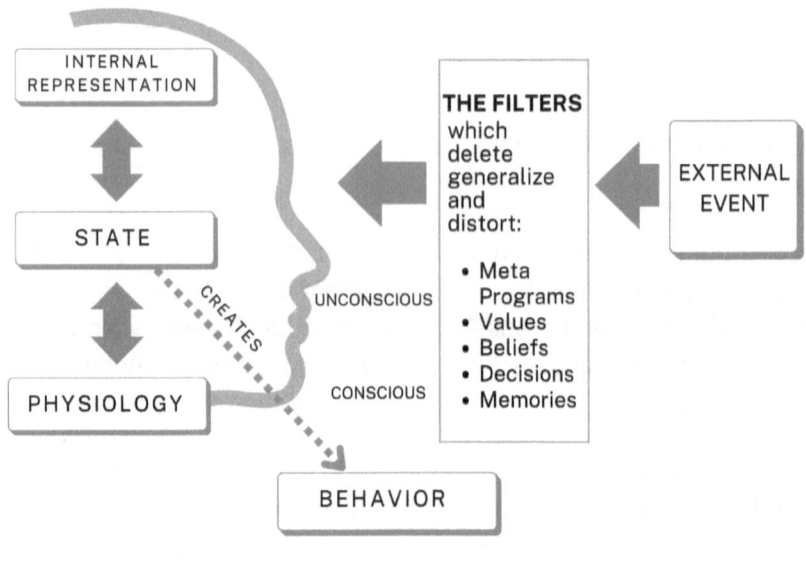

"The Map is not the territory" is a phrase coined by the Polish-American philosopher and engineer Alfred Korzybski that's commonly used in Neuro Linguistic Programming (NLP). He used it to convey the fact that people often confuse models of reality with reality itself. According to Korzybski, models stand to represent things, but they are not identical to those things.

In other words, everything is subjective, not objective. Everything that gets perceived is based on the individual's perception.

We live inside the world inside our head, not inside the world directly. This is a really big key to understanding what's really happening in your own mind, but also in the minds of people around you.

It helps so much with leadership, with our teams running a business, competitors, clients, customers, projects, everything. Because everyone lives their values, no matter if they like them or not, no matter whether they're aware of them or not. Everyone is motivated by their values and their perceptions are going to be influenced by their past.

At some point along our timeline, be it in a past life, in utero, at birth or at an early stage in this life, we form beliefs that then influence us for our whole lifetime. If, for example, our own birth experience was rough to start with and we weren't put into our mum's arms straight away (skin on skin), but instead were taken away to get measured and washed etc., we might have instantly locked in a belief about the world being a cold and nasty place. We might have thought, "I don't like it here. I don't want to be here."

Our brain always looks for evidence for existing beliefs. (Note: Never do we automatically look for evidence to prove our beliefs wrong!) Therefore, we most likely would have experienced a heap of hardship in our life to prove our initial belief right!

Once another bad thing happens, our subconscious will then respond along the lines of, *"See? I told you so! The world is a cold and nasty place!"*

That's how easy it is for a negative pattern in our life to start — based on what we subconsciously believe. It's irrelevant when the belief was first formed (past life, in utero, birth or during this lifetime) and when the possibly traumatic event happened. We usually can't remember most of these events, in an attempt by our subconscious to keep us 'safe'. Instead, our subconscious, and therefore our body, as a representation of our subconscious, stores all of this information for us, until we are ready to face and release what we've been holding on to.

The important thing here is to know that these subconscious beliefs can be shifted, trauma released, and perceptions changed, and positive beliefs can be locked in instead, so a totally different reality can be created. Therefore, don't worry about all those negative beliefs you might be holding. Believe me, we all have lots of them!

There are many ways to shift them, for example with NLP (Neuro Linguistic Programming), Holographic Kinetics, hypnosis, tapping, kinesiology, *Take The Brakes Off*™ *(Self-) Clearing Method* and *The Ultimate Breakthrough*

Journey (my version of *The Spiral*), to name a few. I've personally used and experienced tons of them with great results.

However, when it comes to clearing lifetimes of emotional baggage, conditioning and upper limits (in short: creating a paradigm shift), connecting with your highest truth and deeply embodying the shifts, and therefore laying the foundation to becoming unstoppable in your full expression, living your purpose and creating wealth, whilst making the biggest impact possible, I've never found anything as potent and fast as the maps, frames and techniques I use with *The Ultimate Breakthrough Journey* (my version of *The Spiral*).

Its objective is to clear the largest amount of baggage within the shortest amount of time. Combined with my fine-tuned intuition and in depth understanding of spirit, Universal Law, consciousness, our body, as well as running a (purpose-driven) business, I've been honoured to witness mind-blowing results for my clients time and time again. People shift deeply held beliefs and perceptions that had created their life and experience up to the point of working together – all in a matter of moments, opening them up to experience more alignment, embodiment and possibilities than ever before.

For a complete list of current programs I offer, please visit my website www.sandmew.com.

So, what do we take from this knowledge?

Awareness. Awareness that we have patterns and beliefs that are way deeper than our conscious mind can ever access. Awareness that we need to acknowledge the point in time when the belief was formed in the first place, so we can understand and let go of holding onto it. Our subconsciousness (and therefore our nervous system and body) tries to hold onto the memory with all its might, so we don't forget it before we've received the lesson/ learning/ message from it.

The beauty is that our brain is continuously trying to make the subconscious conscious. This allows us to come more and more into our authentic self, so we can drop the judgement to self and others, take our power back internally, centre back into our authentic being and create our life in alignment with our truth. Therefore, triggers are actually an opportunity to grow.

I know, triggers can be very intense and usually don't feel good. However, they are always an opportunity to grow. We can go deeper into the pain, the struggle, the shadow, and actually alchemize what's there. Then we can expand from there and ultimately raise our consciousness level. And like I said, that's where all the magic happens.

Many years ago I had the honour of being introduced to some Elders. They confirmed to me that time is running out for humanity to make the drastic changes required to keep our earth in balance. In fact, at the time they said we only had exactly 11 years left and that the Earth literally required humanity to "not move a feather" during this time; meaning, everything from driving cars, producing plastics and pollution had to stop. Unfortunately, this is now already many years ago and, as you well know, humanity hasn't stopped.

This may sound threatening and scary. And in many ways, it is. However, there is no point in going into powerlessness and losing hope. Going into fear and freeze response is not going to bring the change we may want and need to see in the world.

What we can do however, is focus on our own inner journey, our own rise in consciousness and evolution.

You may think that that is not going to be enough and make that much of a difference, however, I beg to differ. According to Dr Hawkins, who came up with the Scale of Consciousness that I mentioned previously, to become more conscious is the greatest gift anyone can give to the world. He has calculated the various levels of human awareness, which range from shame, guilt and dogma around 20-50, to courage at 200 and unconditional love at 500, to enlightenment and purpose at 700-1000, as illustrated in Part 1 - Chapter 'Allostatic Load'.

These numbers were calibrated through millions of kinesiological tests on thousands of people during more than 20 years of research and released with his book "Power vs Force", introducing kinesiology and the Scale of Consciousness to the world in 1995.

The realisation that we as people, as humanity, can go for our desires and really shift the state of the world is life changing. Every single individual's awakening to this understanding is pivotal and contributes in a way bigger sense than what is perceivable at first sight.

Every individual counts. Because we are all interconnected, any individual's increase in consciousness also raises to some degree the consciousness of everyone on the planet. According to Dr David Hawkins, although only 15% of the world's population is above the critical consciousness level of 200, the collective power of that 15% has the weight to counterbalance the negativity of the remaining 85%.

"The power of the relatively few individuals near the top of the consciousness scale counterbalances the weaknesses of the masses toward the bottom to achieve the overall average of 204. (...) The way to enhance our power in the world is by increasing our integrity, understanding and capacity for compassion," says Dr. David Hawkins.

The Effect of One Highly Conscious Individual
by Dr David Hawkins

Kinesiological testing has shown that:

One individual at...

level 700* counterbalances 70 million individuals below level 200.

level 600 counterbalances 10 million individuals below level 200.

level 500 counterbalances 750,000 individuals below level 200.

level 400 counterbalances 400,000 individuals below level 200.

level 300 counterbalances 90,000 individuals below level 200.

Twelve individuals at level 700* equals one Avatar at 1,000.

As of 1995, there were 12 persons on the planet who calibrated at 700.

What that means is that if you do the work; you look inwards, shift your own state, clear your baggage and raise your level of consciousness, it will have a ripple effect around you. No matter if you talk to people directly or not, you'll positively impact approximately 90k+ people in a radius around you. The number gets exponentially larger, the higher your level of consciousness.

We have the power to change our life and create our reality, rather than being totally exposed to random happenings. We aren't helpless. Fragile as humans, yes, but not powerless. I'm all about empowering people with the knowledge and skills around how to shift stuff and tap into ultimate possibilities. When we know how to use this power of creation, we can rewire our belief systems and mindset to one that attracts and creates positive change in our life - and all around us. We can gain the ability to respond to situations with consciousness. Only when we take full self-responsibility, and take aligned action, can we truly make a difference. This in turn can then have a beneficial ripple effect into the world.

Therefore, pay attention to what you are experiencing in your life. Look for recurring patterns, as they can give you clues about whether you have locked in some healthy positive beliefs or negative ones that are setting you up for hardship and failure.

In saying that, it's important not to be too hard on yourself with this understanding. It's easy to judge yourself once you know how everything is linked. If you still struggle shifting it despite all the work you've done on yourself up until this point, it's easy to fall into forms of self-loathing or being down on yourself for "still not getting it".

Remember there might be more to the picture; it might be about timing, or that you just haven't found quite the right pathway for you yet. Keep working on yourself, go deeper, trust and never ever give up.

Key Takeaways:

- Our brain processes 400 billion calculations per second, of which only 40 billion get processed via the conscious mind. You then make decisions and take actions based on your neuro-associations, meta programs, beliefs and values.

- "The Map is not the territory." People often confuse models of reality with reality itself, however, anything we experience is simply a mirror of our internal environment.

- Our brain always looks for evidence for existing beliefs. (Note: Never do we automatically look for evidence to prove our beliefs wrong. Therefore, if you have negative or limited ones, watch out!) The beauty is that our brain is continuously trying to make the subconscious conscious.

- It only takes one individual at a consciousness level of 300 in order to positively impact 90k+ other humans, and one individual at 700 to counterbalance 70 million individuals below 200. Every individual's rise in consciousness counts to make the world a better place.

TRAUMA AND TRIGGERS

What is a trigger? To answer that question, we first need to understand trauma a little bit more. Trauma is an emotional response to a terrible event like an accident, rape, or natural disaster. However, it's important to understand that we can also get traumatised by events that don't get labelled as 'highly traumatic' or 'terrible'. Trauma is very subjective to the individual. As a rule of thumb, trauma happens whenever we experience an event that we can't process properly at the time when it happens.

Immediately after a very traumatic event, shock and denial are typical. Longer term reactions include unpredictable emotions, flashbacks, strained relationships, and even physical symptoms like headaches or nausea. However, trauma can also stay dormant for a long time, with the individual not necessarily being aware of its presence until a trigger brings it to the surface again.

The more traumatically you experience an event, the more likely it is that your mind doesn't store it as a whole event on the timeline in your memory, but instead as scattered pieces all over your brain, much like a shattered porcelain plate. These porcelain pieces can get triggered at any given time with experiences, comments, smells, or the sound of music.

This explains why a client of mine who lost her husband in an accident a few years ago had this intense moment of waking up to the scream of a bird one day. She nearly vomited in response. This bird only migrates through her area at a specific time of the year. She called it "her bird" and it reminded her of the anniversary getting close. It brought up all the feelings of the dark night of her soul again. Feelings originating when she found out about the death of her beloved partner.

The triggers will bring up whatever got locked in and trapped in your body at the time of the traumatic event. Then it's much like experiencing the moment again, even though you might not even have a clear memory of it. You might feel all of a sudden really scared, and you're shaking all over, but you don't even know why. That's because nothing seems to be going on right in that moment that would give a plausible explanation for what's come up. You might have had a memory trigger of a traumatic experience come up, from when you were younger, that you had totally suppressed because it was too big to process at the time.

This is also the reason why we can go into a kitchen and smell a certain scent, and it can bring up either good or bad memories of childhood.

The triggers can also bring up anxiety, intense emotions, and potentially your go-to trauma-response or stress pattern, which is either fight, flight or freeze. This will determine whether you typically go into action and 'doing' mode (fight), run away (flight) or get so tired that you need to have a nap on the couch to be able to continue your day (freeze).

You might get annoyed, want to run away, or you withdraw and shut down. It depends on your own personal patterns and how they show up for you. However, the main point is the invitation to become curious. You can ask yourself questions such as:

- What's playing out?
- What's coming up for me?
- What just happened?
- What just drained me?

Just start asking those questions to become familiar with your own patterns of resistance and triggers.

Now, please don't get disheartened, if it feels like you've cleared or addressed so much already, but there still seem to be many triggers and layers coming up for you. You are a multi-dimensional being and having "stuff" in our subconscious memory is totally normal. See these triggers as opportunities to clear stuff that would otherwise remain unnoticed. It's like someone who is holding a torch at a door in the dark, that would otherwise have been missed. Now you've got the chance to open it, look at what's behind it and choose how you'll respond. Will it be the same as in the past?

As mentioned before, *The Ultimate Breakthrough Journey* (my version of *The Spiral*) offers the most systematic approach that I've ever come across, as it's designed to clear the largest amount of emotional baggage in the least amount of time possible - with mind blowing results. I personally find that when we can acknowledge the past, including past lives and ancestral lineages and what set up the trauma in the first place, we can also free ourselves from future cycles of similarities — ultimately setting us free. To achieve this freedom, we see everything we need to understand and integrate as part of it in order to heal and replace it. Afterwards, the same triggers create a totally different response. You can then respond calmly and in a centred way to the same events/people/situations that you would've felt totally triggered by without the clearing/healing.

Whatever pathway or modality you choose depends entirely on you and your own preferences. You'll know, if you listen deeply within, just as much as you'll know which practitioner to go to.

Key Takeaways:

- Trauma is very subjective to the individual and happens whenever we experience an event that we can't process properly at the time when it happens. It then gets stored in our system as trapped emotions, beliefs, etc.

- Triggers will bring up whatever got locked in and trapped in our body at the time of the traumatic event, including but not limited to anxiety, intense emotions, as well as a fight, flight or freeze response. They can happen anytime, even decades or lifetimes later.

- With specific modalities and tools, trauma can get cleared and healed by the root cause, which can then also free ourselves from future cycles of similarities — ultimately setting us free.

UNIVERSAL LORE AND INTERFERENCES

The reason why this work is so effective is that we don't just acknowledge the body, mind, subconscious, brain and nervous system. We also acknowledge Universal Lore and energetics.

This is where you may feel like it's getting a bit "woo woo". However, it is really about how our universe works and matter is created. If we don't acknowledge and work with it, simply because it feels unknown (and therefore scary) to our mind, we miss the very point and will forever keep on being stuck in the same loops.

First of all, you are a multidimensional being. Universal Lore or so-called Lores are the building blocks of our existence. Underpinning the rules of Lore are the 12 universal laws which interact and create realities exponentially, with cause and effect cycling through time and space all along attracting the same.

The 12 universal laws are:

- The law of attraction
- The law of vibration
- The law of correspondence
- The law of Cause and effect
- The law of Divine oneness
- The law of compensation
- The law of polarity
- The law of inspired action
- The law of relativity
- The law of gender
- The law of perpetual transmutation of energy
- The law of rhythm

Until we understand these laws and how they interplay to create Lore, we will forever be playing in someone else's game.

Discussing each and every one of these concepts would turn this book into many. Moreover, Lore takes these 12 universal laws to an entirely next level and is based on ancient knowledge that hasn't been spoken or written about all that much yet.

I'd like to share a few relevant concepts with you to explain some of the frames that are integral to this work. They are based on the ancient knowledge which I've studied, explored and practised for decades. They've not only created mind-blowing results in my own life but also thousands of lives of my clients. I'm sharing a little introduction to them with you today in the hope that they may illuminate areas for you, you may have not explored before on the quest to take the brakes off and unlock your potential (and the ones of your businesses and projects).

As mentioned, we are multidimensional beings whose dimensional universe can entrap other dimensions and in turn be trapped by others. According to this ancient knowledge, all memories of these dimensions are locked in the soul and reflected in the body and only the creator of the dimension can change it, which is you in this case (with the support of a practitioner who understands Lore).

The consequences of the choices and decisions we make can cycle throughout eternity (that means over many lifetimes) until we bring them back into balance.

The Lore of Free Will, for example, says that everything in existence has the right to free will and choice. Every being has the right to travel through time and space as an observer, free from interference.

However, if you enter a dimension of another through your free will, including agreements of entrapment, you are then governed by the laws of that dimension. This includes entering someone else's house, business, office or shop, or if you go out and see someone else for dinner at their place. It also includes partaking in someone else's course, mastermind or conference. If you step into someone else's space, you step into what's referred to as their "game" which is defined by their intent and integrity. If we are not energetically aware and the intent isn't set well, this can have detrimental effects on you and your being.

Moreover, much like in traditional Chinese medicine (TCM), Universal Lore sees us as energy beings. Energy has the free right to flow as kinetic energy (Chi in TCM). We create an imbalance by trapping energy through our thoughts and intent which can create energetic blockages and disconnect certain body parts and organs from free flowing "communication" with each other. As mentioned under the chapter "Trapped Emotions," this potential energy can grow into disease or another form of entity.

This is due to another Lore which is worth mentioning. When someone agrees to integrate with another, a new entity or dimension is created by the joint agreement and intent of both. The reality of a separate dimension is created this way; for example, when spirit and soul integrate, their agreement and intent can create a body.

Therefore, if an emotion gets experienced really strongly or persistently, it might lead to an entity being formed as a result. This can be created in you (internally) or someone else (externally created) and live in your or someone else's body. It's like your emotion takes on a lifeform on its own. And you might end up doing something or behaving in a way that feels 'alien' or foreign to you. As if you weren't yourself.

All agreements are valid eternally, unless dissolved with the right knowledge and techniques.

Therefore, if an emotion gets experienced really strongly or persistently, it might lead to an entity being formed as a result which then either lives on in your own body, internally created, or someone else's, or it gets created in somebody else, but lives on in you, externally created.

Entities can be felt like persistent and intense emotions that keep coming back and grip you totally unexpectedly, or they can feel a bit like brain fog. It totally depends on the emotion, entity and experience. Persistent intense feelings and brain-fog are just a couple of commonly perceived signs that an entity is present and playing havoc.

Once discovered, it's time to clear it with your intent and command and to reclaim your body's space, which is your vehicle, as it's only meant to be inhibited by yourself and your own higher self and spirit alone.

Signs of having inter-dimensionals 'on board' are:

- Extreme tiredness
- Literally feeling knocked out
- Things going pear-shaped in your life
- Acting or feeling totally out of sorts
- Your eyes not looking clear
- Sickness
- Feeling very intense
- Feeling swamped
- Unable to ground and centre yourself properly

Ideally, we want to be an observer. An observer is someone who is non-reactive, centred and at the same time open-hearted and compassionate, without "taking stuff on" (ie. without getting affected by things). In other words: Someone who has cleared their baggage!

The most straightforward way to not take stuff on and be in your centre is by practising to be 100% in your body and present.

Being "out of body" can be due to many reasons, including:

- Trapped emotions
- Beliefs causing cognitive dissonance
- Taking stuff on from others or the environment
- Trauma being activated from past dimensions
- Interdimensionals: Human Spirits, Entities or Interferences that are "on board" and are literally taking up space in your body, preventing you from being able to come back in.

So how do we end up with Interdimensionals? Any time we are 'wide open' energetically, we may unconsciously open ourselves up to taking stuff on.

This may be due to one or more of the following:

- A dysregulated nervous system
- Trauma
- Immense pain that may lead to us 'dreaming ourselves away'
- Drugs
- Alcohol
- Other nervous system altering substances
- Stress
- Distraction
- Childbirth

We may also take on stuff far more easily than others when we have many open centres in Human Design. If you're familiar with your Design and Chart, which is readily available on the internet, as long as you know your birth date and time of birth, and you notice a few open centres, it can certainly help a lot to familiarise yourself with techniques to stay in your body. This is where my motto comes in: When you're in your centre, nothing else can enter.

It's also important to know that we may entrap ourselves when we ask an external force or energy for guidance and help (as opposed to our own spirit or the universe).

A huge factor to take into account when working with symbols, guides, angels, or any other external forces, powers and rituals — which is so very common in the New Age world and Religion alike — is that they may entrap our will, block us from being fully in our body and/or influence and hold us back from living our purpose.

Not every being, just because it's wrapped in white light, angel wings or goddess statues, and has been prayed to for centuries or millennia, has a good intent. Intent is more than being clear on what it is you want to manifest or achieve. Remember that thoughts are also energy and your "true intent" behind any action will be subject to cause and effect. You can't hide your true intent.

Just because a lot of people say it's the right thing, or a good thing to pray to Archangel Michael, for example, doesn't mean it's necessarily right or right for you. It's still just a man-made construct, which can lead to entrapment and therefore to a disempowered state of yourself.

Interdimensionals don't even necessarily have to be "bad". On the contrary, I believe that everything/everyone is intrinsically good: everything/everyone deep down just wants to be loved, seen and acknowledged. However, everything/everyone has its own personal purpose which simultaneously is an agenda. They may not be good or bad, they simply may not overlap with yours, and therefore take you away from living your purpose and potential.

What are Interdimensionals, i.e. Entities and Interferences?

As described earlier, entities and interferences are energies or beings in space. To clarify exactly what this means, please go over the previous pages again.

According to Universal Lore there are quite a few different variations, however, for the sake of ease, I usually simply differentiate between the following ones:

- Animal Spirits: If you've killed an animal (in this or past life), it's got the right to "hop onboard" and stay there, until released. Sometimes the spirit of an animal also hops on board (or into your space), because it's got a message for you (positive or negative) or has been invited by you. Again, use the greatest level of caution, as you never know its truest intent.

- Human Spirits: Exactly as above, just with humans.

- Entities (internally or externally created): We create an imbalance by trapping energy through our thoughts and intent which can create energetic blockages and disconnect certain body parts and organs from free flowing "communication" with each other. This potential energy can grow into dis-ease or another form of entity.

  If an emotion gets experienced really strongly or persistently, it might lead to an entity being formed as a result which then either lives on in your own body, internally created, or someone else's, or it gets created in somebody else, but lives on in you, externally created.

- Interferences: Beings/ life/ energy forms from different places that don't have a body to act out their agenda. Therefore, they take up the opportunity to hop onboard an "empty body" whenever possible.

  This is one of the main reasons why it is so important to be 100% in your body!
  It's for your own energetic safety and wellbeing.

You can see, either through ignorance, free choice or stress, entities or interferences from other dimensions can enter your world by way of agreement or contract, that then affect and influence your world. Once they've entered your world, they'll take up space within you, which leads to you not being able to fully be 100% present in your body anymore.

Key Takeaways:

- Universal Lore or so-called Lores are the building blocks of our existence. Underpinning the rules of Lore are the 12 universal laws which interact and create realities exponentially, with cause and effect cycling through time and space all along attracting the same.

- We are multidimensional beings whose dimensional universe can entrap other dimensions and in turn be trapped by others. Either through ignorance, free choice or stress, entities or interferences from other dimensions can enter your world by way of agreement or contract, that then affect and influence your world and ability to live your purpose and potential. All agreements are valid eternally, unless dissolved with the right knowledge and techniques.

- The most straightforward way to not take (more) stuff and Interdimensionals on and be in your centre, is by practising to be 100% in your body, present and 'the observer'.

PART 2

LEADING FROM CENTRE

BEING "IN BODY" AND CENTRE VERSUS "OUT OF BODY" AND CENTRE

As I mentioned, once someone is "out of body", their goal needs to be to come back into their body and centre. We can achieve this by setting a clear, deliberate intention. We need to claim our body back and be firm and assertive.

The solution to getting affected by crowds and other people:
Be 100% present in your Body

Our Body is like a glass.

If you don't fill it 100% with your Spirit/Higher Self/Presence, the gap will be filled with whatever else is around you in the room (smelly air, stuffy energy from arguments & tension, other people's emotions/feelings/entities/ interferences/projections; in short: 'stuff')

>>> You'll feel highly affected by everyone else around you (the story of an empath).

The Solution to getting affected by everyone else around you:
Fill your glass (body) all the way to the top with you (your Spirit/higher self/presence). Don't leave a gap!

Use the following affirmation with firm intention:

"I (your full name) command my higher self & Spirit to be 100% in my body on all levels and dimensions"

When we've got 'stuff on board', when trauma has been reactivated, when trapped emotions are stirred up, or a past dimension is triggered, we won't be able to bring ourselves fully back into our body and centre without clearing. Depending on what's come up, we can do clearing either through self-clearing and/or potentially with the support of a knowledgeable, Lore-aware practitioner.

To give you an idea of how much people are generally in their body, here is what some kinesiological tests and research have shown: On average, Australians are about 8% in their bodies, Americans about 6% and Germans about 4%. Other countries vary. Generally speaking, no matter where we look, the percentage is quite low.

Some underlying contributing factors for this are collective trauma from wars and the general history of the country, as well as how regulated, physically and emotionally present people are based on their culture and belief systems.

I'm not sharing these concepts and statistics with you in order to worry you, but to raise your awareness, so you can make sure you're in your body and hold a strong energetic frame in your own life and field.

Unfortunately, I see so many leaders, health practitioners, coaches and mentors out in the world who've got stuff onboard, who are not embodied and don't lead from their centre. This then doesn't only affect their life and experience of *their* reality, but also that of everyone around them and it influences their decisions, which potentially affect a lot of people (i.e. their followers, teams, organisations, networks, clubs, etc and of course their loved ones).

Apart from making sure we're "in body", we also need to make sure we're in centre and lead from there. There are many reasons why we get "pulled out of centre". In the following image, which was originally published in my bestseller *Remember Who You Are,* you can see a few of them listed where the arrows are pointing away from the centre:

Out of Centre
forgetting to/ not knowing how to/
not being able to hold your own space at the same time

Outcomes such as making sure everyone is happy, striving for acceptance/money/ job/freedom etc ("once I've got xyz I'll be happy")

Stuck in the head, WORRY, trying to control outcomes, FEAR

following someone else's/society's values/expectations & forgetting about your own ones

Empathically feeling into someone else

Codependant Relationship

Your Centre
most authentic state, 100% spirit embodied,
being the observer, at point zero,
making sure all your 3-5 core values = needs are met,
(Note: this does NOT mean shutting off!
On the contrary, it's a wide open heart space!)

Everything feels solid, safe, certain, peaceful, calm,
on track & how it is meant to be
Even when things are going 'wrong' and drama is happening on the outside,
you don't lose your centre, the place of inner certainty within
and the knowing that all is well no matter what.

© Sand Mew

In your centre, 100% spirit / potential-embodied, you're in your most authentic state. There, you are at point zero, the observer. From this space, we make sure that all our three to five core values are met as needs. We'll be discussing our values and how they shape our reality in the coming chapters.

Being at point zero does NOT mean shutting off or resigning from feeling emotions. Quite the opposite. We just step back from the drama and charge attached to things. We are fully in our centre and not attached, but at ease. We have a strong spine and an open heart space. In this space, everything feels solid, safe, certain, peaceful, calm and on track, even when things are happening that feel out of control or don't fit into our idea of how things should be.

When we don't lose our centre and place of inner certainty, and know that all is well, no matter what, we know we are in our centre and body.

When we're out of centre (and potentially "out of body"), on the contrary, which is indicated at the top of the image, we might be experiencing one or more of the following:

- Forgetting or not knowing how to hold our space
- Getting stuck in the head, worrying and trying to control outcomes
- Feeling fearful
- Following someone else's (or society's) values and expectations and forgetting about our own ones
- Being in a codependent relationship, getting pulled out of centre
- Trying to make sure everyone's happy
- Striving for acceptance, love, money, a specific job or result etc without feeling at peace at the same time ("Once I've got ...., then I'll be happy")
- Empathetically feeling into someone else and getting triggered by ("sucked into") whatever they're telling us

Here are some of the direct benefits that fully embodying your spirit and potential, plus leading from centre will have on you:

- Clarity and calm
- Energy and vitality
- Resilience
- Grounded and centred
- Inner peace
- Knowing yourself
- Self-responsibility
- Protection for others
- Magnetism

Looking after your own energetic game and inner integrity, is your own responsibility. It won't help blaming others for it, or what's happened to you. That will only give it or them your power. As I mentioned previously, what's happened to you and what you're feeling and experiencing is not your fault. It's just your responsibility to do something about it.

Once you've claimed yourself back - with support if needed - you'll be feeling all the more centred, stable, certain, confident, safe and thriving for it. Your decisions will be based on alignment, care and the highest good, rather than emotions, pain bodies and imbalances. When living and leading from centre, every action carries a positive ripple and life is a positive experience of ease, peace and possibilities.

Key Takeaways:

- Continually focus on being in your body and centre at all times, so you can be in alignment, focused, calm, clear and confident, and make decisions that not only feel good but will also make the biggest positive impact possible.

- When we've either got 'stuff on board' and/or when trauma has been reactivated, trapped emotions are stirred up or even a past dimension triggered, we won't be able to bring ourselves back fully without clearing.

- Looking after your own energetic game and inner integrity, is your own responsibility (self clearing and potentially with the support of a knowledgeable, Lore-aware practitioner).

---

6 DAILY SELF CARE PRACTICES

In order to live from centre and experience life with ease, you need sound daily habits and rituals. The ideas offered here will help you make sound decisions, become more self-aware, take responsibility, and not get swept into emotional rollercoasters, trigger volcanoes or downward spirals. Moreover, these practices help to balance out busy times with time out in which you don't need to look after anyone but yourself. This allows you to listen inwards, receive and be open to your own (higher) truth, which you then can communicate to the world. All of which is resulting in you being a better version of yourself to be around.

Before your subconscious needs to send you intense messages, such as severe stress, overwhelm, frantic busy-ness or sickness, it pays off for you to stop and listen. Believe me, I had to learn this the hard way quite a few times over the course of my journey. I've run businesses for many years whilst having little ones, a connected relationship, a highly inspired, visionary mind that longs to create, coupled with a strong desire and need to listen to my body.

Here are 6 tips to stay healthy, well and balanced, in order to optimally support yourself through busy times:

- **Get proper sleep.**
  The number one way to maintain wellbeing, a great immune system, strong nerves and happiness is, sleep. How much exactly you need to feel good and keep up over the long term depends on you and your body. Some people love to sleep and process their whole life like this. They might sleep 9–10 hours a night. Generally, a healthy amount for the body to rest and revive overnight is 8 hours.

- **Keep up a nutritious and healthy diet.**
  An alive, well balanced and, if possible, organic diet is a must to keep our bodies working well and keep them healthy. Whilst it's great to have lots of fresh fruit and veggies, it's important to remember that

it's protein that sustains our energy over prolonged periods of time. Remember to start the day with a proper breakfast, including some sort of protein (vegan, vegetarian or animal sources), so it can provide you with lots of energy for the first half of the day.

On top of that, fermented foods assist with a healthy gut flora. Our gut flora has a direct link to our brain. More and more scientific studies are showing that those with lots of healthy beneficial bacteria in their digestive system are way less prone to depression, mental conditions and disease in general — in short, a balanced state of mind, body and being will be the reward.

- **Drink LOTS of water.**
  H2O is a must for the body to function. It's so easy to forget that the body is made up of 55–60% water and that water is vital for it to keep functioning. Sometimes we get sweet cravings, sore ears, headaches, attention problems, tiredness, etc. all just because we are actually thirsty! Make it easy for your body and kidneys, by providing it with clear pure, filtered water (fluoride free).

- **Keep moving.**
  Our bodies are made to move and jiggle! There's a reason kids naturally never sit still. We are meant to move to keep flexible. Do whatever it takes to make you move at least 10–20 minutes a day to release good amounts of endorphins (our happy hormones).

  Stretching our meridians helps us to release all associated emotions and hormones and therefore helps us let go of all sorts of stuff that no longer serves us. Stomping out all excess tension can be like a brain dump, if used in the right way — leaving you feeling refreshed and tons lighter!

- **Breathe deeply.**
  Do you know that so many people hold their breath? Do you breathe deeply, so that your belly moves up and down? By breathing right into your belly, you give your lungs the chance to fully empty and refill with fresh new air, allowing oxygen to be circulated around your body much more easily. Your diaphragm gets the chance to release and relax, which in turn has a beneficial effect on your Solar Plexus nerve centre and stomach just underneath it. Both of these are directly associated with your mood and when you are feeling anxious,

stressed and tense, moving your diaphragm can instantly help release the anxiety and tension.

Releasing the tension in your Solar Plexus can also easily be done by applying pressure to its associated reflex in your hands, ears and feet. This has an "unlocking" effect on your diaphragm and a relaxing effect on your stomach, giving you the chance to relax, digest foods and situations properly and handle life in general a whole lot better. For access to a free mini Reflexology training about the *Power of Feet*, visit *www.TheFootprintConnection.com*

- **Check in with yourself regularly.**
  Make sure you get a proper amount of time off each week in which you do meditation or some other form of deep self-reflection and centring. I personally aim to meditate every or every second morning on waking, do self-clearing several times daily, which I utilise as a process to check in with my spirit / potential and inner knowing, and make sure I'm fully activated and present in my body before I face the world. These check-ins involve Take The Brakes Off™ - Self Clearing, listening within, grounding myself, checking the way I stand and distribute my weight, adjusting my energy and much more.

These self-care techniques help keep me feeling totally centred, calm, at peace, inspired, trusting and in the flow — in harmony with myself and the world, no matter what's going on — and without taking more than a few seconds or minutes at a time!

I know that sometimes it's not easy to find this time for yourself unless it's a non-negotiable, and even then it can be tricky, especially when you're a parent or care for others who demand your constant attention. Self-care easily gets put last, however, in doing so you signal to your Limitless Potential that you don't see "it" and that "it" is not important to you. Which in turn leads to it getting even harder to remember who you are and reconnect ...

Self-care time such as meditating, doing yoga or walking on the beach can then turn into a "chore", yet another thing you have to do, despite knowing that the activities will, or should feel good. Getting yourself to do them may be a battle, exhausting and bring so much resistance with them that it might almost be a relief not getting the time for them at all or getting distracted whilst doing them.

Does this sound familiar?

This type of battle can come up when there is a deep truth within you that a part of you is scared to know about, hear or see. In which case, you might sabotage yourself or even experience spouts of anxiety.

Alternatively, there might be a part of you that's scared to not "get anywhere", when you finally take the time out for yourself.

The lack of inner connection might result in you feeling restless and too under pressure to utilise your time well that it seems like a waste of time when you end up sitting and making the effort but hear or feel nothing. The responsibility to be there for everyone else, your business and / or your family is so big that you can't even give yourself or your higher self the time to reveal itself to you. In this state it almost seems like a luxury to listen inwards, which is nonsense of course, but very real for the person feeling like that.

I find that it's easier to shift the self-criticising thoughts of being selfish when taking time out, or giving back to yourself, when you acknowledge the fact that you are actually giving back to your body as your temple and your potential — not really to yourself in a selfish sense.

The way I see it, your ego refers to the little child within you that gets frightened when you want to leave your comfort zone, as it fears you abandoning it. Therefore, it tries to distract you from and talk you out of any changes that could lead to a more expanded and self-loving state.

Your ego doesn't represent your higher self. It comes from fear. If you live from a disconnected place, as in disconnected from your higher self and truth, and the opposite of spirit and potential embodied, you feel disconnected from others and can't empathise with them. You experience fear, act from your mind and try to control everything to keep up a false sense of security.

On the other hand, the more integrated and embodied you are, the more you honour your deepest truth. This in turn builds trust in yourself and the universe, increasing your sense of certainty. As a result, you more deeply honour everyone else and the world at the same time. The path inwards, to yourself, and being able to stay there, is therefore really the foundation you need, to be able to deeply and authentically connect with the world.

Key Takeaways:

- In order to stay in centre with much more ease, you need to have sound daily habits and rituals in place that keep you balanced and functioning optimally, with a strong sense of certainty.

- Self-care easily gets put last, however, in doing so you signal to your Limitless Potential that you don't see "it" and that "it" is not important to you, resulting in self-sabotage and feeling overwhelmed, unsupported and disconnected.

- Giving back to your body as our temple and vehicle and our potential is not selfish but selfless, as you become a better version of yourself and can make a much bigger positive impact.

YOUR VALUES AND HOW THEY SHAPE YOUR REALITY

Our values are key to understanding our motivations and perceptions, but also to bring us back to ourselves, into centre and get our needs met. To understand our values means we have the power to create an inspired life. A truly inspired life, a really aligned life, and understanding other people with much more compassion and accuracy.

The way we perceive life is in the form of polar opposites. We have certain feelings and states of being that we despise, disapprove of and judge. We have others that we want to feel and that are really important to us. The latter feelings are referred to as values. They might be deep connection, family time, honesty, authenticity, beauty, travel or wealth. Whatever they are, they are something that we highly desire or we really like, and which are really important to us. Without them we wouldn't feel good or happy in our life, relationships or in our workplace.

The values of a business owner are not going to be the same ones as the ones of a young single person travelling the world. The same goes for a high school student versus a parent of young kids, or when you're an elderly person nearing the end of your lifetime. Different aspects of life, traits and outcomes are going to be important for you, depending on where you're at in life. Your motivations and drivers will be different. Therefore, your values will most likely change over the course of your lifetime.

Knowing your values will enable you to know why you like the things you like and understand your motivations around your choices. It will also give you an understanding into the choices of others around you, your team, clients and family members, and enable you to respond in a more compassionate way, or at least not have unreasonable expectations of yourself and others.

Being clear on what your values are also allows you to adjust them, if you feel like they aren't congruent with where you want to go. We always live our values. They might just not be in alignment with our goals and therefore values that we'd like to have.

For example, if you dream of building wealth and investments, but no matter how much you earn, you never seem to have enough, it can help to assess whether you secretly value beauty (as in clothes, beautifying the house, gadgets or the like), travel, socialising (as in going out for drinks etc) or comfort over wealth creation. You might even have money on your list of top priorities, but if wealth creation isn't, it might just always get spent before it can be built.

Once you've got clarity around your current values and what you truly fill all your time and space with, you can see whether they match your desired outcomes and dreams in your life and tweak them, if necessary. By doing so, you'll find it easier than ever to take the steps that are required to really make your dreams come true.

Note: You're only going to be able to do this, if your desired outcome is YOUR dream, your vision, not someone else's expectation. To decipher what's what, just keep reading. I'll go much deeper into this topic in the following chapters.

Some people think that they're sabotaging. Most likely they're just living their values, which they might not even be aware of. The more aware we become of our values, the more we can guide and create our life and design it in a way that's really aligned. And when we do that, we live a very inspired life, and that's what I'd like for you. Knowing this empowers us to realize that if we want to change the world, we must first change ourselves.

Key Takeaways:

- Our values are a key to understanding our motivations and perceptions (and the ones of others), but also to bring us back to ourselves, into centre and to get our needs met.

- We always live our values. Being clear on what your values are also allows you to adjust them, if you feel like they aren't congruent with where you want to go.

- The more aware we become of our values, the more we can guide and create our life and design it in a way that's really aligned, resulting in a very inspired life.

MIRROR THEORY

Now that we are clear on what values are, let's explore the polar opposite: those feelings and states that we *disapprove* of and that we therefore push away. The ones that don't fit into our value system, or even worse, the ones that work against it.

Unless we become aware of this polarisation and we clear the reaction that we hold in our body towards desperately wanting to pull our values closer, in fear that we might end up on the opposite end of the scale, we will keep manifesting experiences into our life that we don't want. Therefore, holding a fierce wall up against the traits that we disapprove of.

When we disapprove of something or of a feeling, we might even claim that it's not a part of us and literally disown it.

For example, we so want to be kind, loving and compassionate, but definitely not harsh, narcissistic and unethical. So we point the finger at those who we perceive are acting out these traits, and subconsciously or even consciously push them away with vengefulness. You might think, *"How can they do this to us or the world?! I could NEVER do this to others!"*

When we connect with like-minded people, we really like and respect them, and that's because they live by our values.

Take a business mastermind for example. If your values are Growth, Impact, Freedom and Wealth for instance, and you share the table with business owners with the same values, chances are high that you'll connect with the people present and feel inspired.

The better they are at living your values and the more aligned they are to your values, the more highly you'll think of them and you might even put them on a pedestal, depending on whether you feel you live up to your own standards and values or not.

Let's look at what happens when you meet someone who doesn't live by your values. They might be very disconnected, mean to people around them and not interested in changing anything about where they're at. Even worse, they think that they're a victim and take zero self responsibility for their situation.

Well, in that case they don't live by your values and probably a part of you will put them in the ditch. You'll most likely start feeling frustrated listening to them, want to move on and definitely want nothing to do with them. Right? In that case, you subconsciously push them really far away from you. You most likely don't even want to associate with these people.

This is basic human behaviour. We 'pull' people closer who live by our values and 'reject' or 'push people away', if they don't. It depends on how much charge you hold around your values that will determine whether you get literally triggered around them or whether you feel calm and centred in their presence.

This charge around behaviour, emotions, attributes etc that doesn't match our values, then gets stored in our body. Whenever we encounter the same behaviour, attribute or emotion in someone else or even ourselves, we'll respond and judge according to the charge we hold towards it. And we'll be feeling this charge viscerally.

In reality we all have a huge range of emotions and states; they're the same for all of us humans. Some of them we might not like to identify with, however they are all still a part of us. They might just be a suppressed or disowned part of us. Like the people who don't live by our values and that we therefore put into the ditch, it's like we've put that part of ourselves that far out of our view, that we can't even detect it on our radar anymore. We call this a shadow. It can also be an emotion or memory that we rather forget about, because we feel shame, guilt or fear around it. *"What? Angry? I'm not angry. I NEVER get angry!"*

These disowned emotions, memories and states get suppressed, which then makes them show up in random ways. A simple rule of thumb is that if I can see a trait in someone else, I definitely possess that trait within myself. Maybe they're expressing something I'm currently suppressing and repressing. Maybe they're repressing something I'm currently expressing. Maybe what they're doing to others is what I'm doing to myself.

Mirror Theory gives us an opportunity to really look deeper into this. You might know the saying, *"The world around you is a reflection of your inner world"*.

Whatever the trait, emotion or attribute you are suppressing or disowning as shadow in yourself is going to be the very thing that you'll be faced with in your reality. This is so we can see what we are subconsciously holding onto and creating.

Usually there is one of the following 4 'Mirror' options playing out. You either:

- Express the traits in the same way, i.e. a colleague shows up in a very competitive way and you get triggered because you actually do this unknowingly lots too.
- Express them in a parallel area; i.e. a team member never seems to stick to the system, meaning others have to pick up the slack. You get triggered. You might not be doing the same ever, however, it might show up the same way in another area of your life, such as the way you handle your bookkeeping or when it comes to cooking with recipes.
- Never express the traits in the same way, i.e. your partner shows up in a lazy manner, is relaxing on the couch with their feet up, whilst you have to do all the work. You get triggered as you see them as very lazy. Chances are that you don't let yourself rest and be lazy enough (or ever).
- Express the traits you see others displaying towards yourself, i.e. a client treats you in a very rude, disrespectful manner. You might never even think to show up towards your clients in this way, however, maybe it reflects the way you are treating yourself.

And specifically speaking to the common dynamic between Visionaries and Integrators:

For Visionaries[2] that feel limited by others:
If you get triggered about others (ie. your partner or team member(s)) being too limited and 'negative', chances are, you're bypassing limitations within yourself. Check if you're centring and grounding yourself enough, in order for you to be able to see the bigger picture, and both, positive and negative aspects / outcomes. If you're bypassing looking at potential negative outcomes and are not looking into how you'd handle them, chances are that others have to take this responsibility and roll over for you. This will lead to them feeling unheard and potentially get 'naggy', limited and negative. No matter what, it will bring up stressors within the dynamic that could be avoided.

Allow yourself to look at pros and cons of your ideas until you can answer and sit with all outcomes without wanting to rush past the negative ones and pretend they don't exist, out of fear that the other person could destroy your dreams. This way you'll own your own limitations and the charge will be released.

For those Integrators[3] that feel triggered by their risk prone partner (or boss):
If you are triggered about someone else being too risky and never thinking about liabilities and risks, and you're feeling like you have to limit someone else and hold them back in order to feel good again, then ask yourself where you are not ever letting yourself expand into more risky thinking.

Where are you taking over the responsibility of limiting oneself over too much for someone else. Is there possibly a way how you could offer them a

---

[2] "A visionary leader turns vision into reality by creating a vivid image of the target they need to attain and creating a specific strategic plan." (April 2013) Forbes.
"A visionary leader ensures the vision becomes reality by stating clear goals, outlining a strategic plan for achieving those goals and equipping and empowering each member to take action on the plan at the organizational, team and individual levels." (29 Dec 2022) Michiganstateuniversityonline.com.
[3] "An Integrator is a person who orchestrates the major functions of an organization. This is the person who manages day-to-day issues and holds the organization's people, processes, systems, priorities, and strategies together." (4 Aug 2022), The Integrator: A Breakdown of the Role-Rocket Fuel University.com.

bit more of a chance to see that themselves? It's very much a dynamic that plays out with others, but also within ourselves.

Mirror theory is a really fascinating concept. When I first came across it many years ago, I was mind blown, because it gave me such a deep, easy and fast insight into our subconscious without having to guess around so much. It lets us uncover what's really playing out underneath the surface, under the black waters surrounding the iceberg of our conscious mind and neutralise it again.

Our brain will always try to make the subconscious conscious, so we can release it, because having a one-sided view is inauthentic and, according to Dr Demartini, can lead to dis-ease and illness in the body.

Our brain always wants to bring us back to a point where we live most authentically and true to our nature. It will do its best to create scenarios in which you can recognise this lost and disowned aspect of yourself again and claim it back.

Unfortunately, we don't generally learn to look at the world like that. Most of us practise bypassing without being aware of it and keep creating our reality accordingly; in a limited and one-sided way. We are all humans with the whole spectrum of human emotions though. Some of which get expressed more than others, but they are all a part of each and every one of us.

By recognising that we might be expressing this shadow aspect in the way we treat our bookkeeping, underwear or the way we respond to our own needs, we can bring the shadow into light, own it back and release the charge. As a result, we set ourselves free.

There are many ways to journal them out, for example with Shadow Flipping or the Dr Demartini Method. However, if we hold a lot of charge in our body towards the bespoke shadow aspect, we will need to release it from the body to create true freedom. This is where modalities and tools such as *Take The Brakes Off*™ - *Self Clearing* and *The Ultimate Breakthrough Journey* (my version of *The Spiral*) comes in. We can clear the charge around situations, emotions, archetypes, people etc extremely fast and potently.

The result? There won't be any charge left in your body around this topic, as you've owned it back. This results in you not having to create it in your reality anymore (or simply not reacting anymore), ultimately allowing you to create your desired reality with so much more ease.

Key Takeaways:

- We experience the world in polar opposites: our values and 'anti-values': things we disapprove of and judge.

- *"The world around you is a reflection of your inner world"*. Whatever the trait, emotion or attribute you are suppressing or disowning as shadow in yourself is going to be the very thing that you'll be faced with in your reality.

- Unless we become aware of this polarisation and we clear the reaction that we hold in our body towards desperately wanting to pull our values closer, in fear that we might end up on the opposite end of the scale, we will keep manifesting experiences into our life that we don't want.

A LIMITED VERSUS
EXPANDED MINDSET

We constantly filter the world, which is infinitely complex, and look for events and experiences that confirm what we already know to be true. This is the reason why we always play out the same patterns over and over and over again.

Once we form a belief it acts out like a tabletop that we add more and more legs underneath. It will become more and more stable and solid as time progresses. Let's take an example here just to make this a little bit more tangible.

Say you were five, you fell down in an old farmhouse, down a flight of stairs. You fell, rolled down and hit your head. You lied on the ground, and you felt all alone and sad because no one's coming to help you. You were all alone. In that moment, you might lock in a belief. To lock something in means you start believing or you decide something to be true, with a very strong, emotional charge around it. You might lock in that the world is a dark place, that you're all alone, and there is no one that will help you. If you locked in those three beliefs and they got locked into your body with a strong emotional charge, guess what? Your body, your system is designed to loop it over and over and over for you.

What happens is that you grow up, completely forget about the experience described above, turn into an adult, and wonder why your life is constantly throwing you curveballs. In other words, it's constantly reflecting back to you that the world is a dark place and that no one comes to help. You might think that you have to do it all yourself and that you're alone, and it doesn't feel very fun.

Therefore, this belief that was originally formed at five years of age gets constantly proven right throughout life. Every time these proofs come in, this evidence in the form of a table leg, gets added underneath this tabletop. What becomes four legs might later on become 10, 20 or even more legs, until the belief is so solid that it turns into a rock formation. This is the case when we meet older people that are really stuck in their ways and extremely stubborn.

It gets difficult to deal with people who have a rigid mindset as they're not open to learning new things to be true. That is beyond the limitations of their mind. Which is quite crazy to believe really, because the world is so infinite. There are limitless possibilities out there, all the time. And if someone thinks, "This is not possible because I've never seen it before", then that's quite an interesting belief to have. We imply that our human mind has seen and experienced everything there is. Even if we're extremely intelligent, we can't possibly have. Unless we tap into our limitlessness, which knows that there are infinite possibilities out there, we'll forever play within the limitations of our human experience.

To recap, once we form a belief, our subconscious and our brain will never allow us to experience anything that proves this belief wrong. Let that sink in.

So if you decided as a five year old with the example from before that the world is a dark place, that you're all alone and that you've got to do it all by yourself and that no one's there to support you, well then that's a pretty sad existence because even though you might consciously be quite joyful, quite positively minded and equipped. It does not mean that your reality can reflect that back to you. Instead, it will keep on bringing challenges into your life, where you feel ultimately alone and that you'll need to sort it all out by yourself, without support. So we constantly filter the world, which is infinitely complex.

Like I mentioned, we look for events and experiences that confirm what we already believe to be true. This is a large part of why we play out the same patterns over and over and over again. It's also part why clearing one simple emotion, interference, pattern or conditioning, that holds an old belief in its place can allow us to experience a completely different reality and something that we've never thought possible.

It's simply like moving curtains out of the way that have been holding us from seeing something that could be potentially a much larger and expanded possibility. But once we clear stuff, we move these curtains, and we can see and believe it to be possible. This allows us to experience it. We can step into it.

Key Takeaways:

- We constantly filter the world, which is infinitely complex, and look for events and experiences that confirm what we already know to be true.

- Once we form a belief, our subconscious and our brain will never allow us to experience anything that proves this belief wrong.

- This is why clearing one simple emotion, interference, pattern or conditioning that holds an old belief in its place can allow us to experience a completely different reality and something that we've never thought possible.

ALIGNMENT

Now that we've talked about having an expansive mindset, this leads us to a fun next chapter. Get ready to expand your mind and tap into possibility!

Ready? Let's go.

You need to know what you want and truly desire first, in order to be able to take the brakes off, so you can create the life you want to be living and ignite your true potential.

All too often there is one of the following scenarios playing out.

- You feel overwhelmed because your goals seem too big. You don't have a strategy and therefore frequently go into stress mode. (This could result in feeling over-stimulated, going into avoidance mode or feeling numb and shut down.)
- You lack clarity, direction and focus in your life. You might only have a vague idea of where you want to go (or your clarity is non-existent). You don't feel satisfied, fulfilled or inspired. This can then turn into self-doubt or the belief that you won't ever get to where you want to.
- You have clear goals, but they don't excite you. You're frequently in "I can't be bothered" mode or feel overwhelmed and spin your wheels.

If this is you, don't worry. All it takes is you knowing what you truly want to focus on; then you can create an aligned strategy that will help you focus, clear out of the way that's blocking you or the outcome and get there.

However, for some this is the trickiest part: knowing what you really truly want and desire — not just what you THINK you want, but actually what lights your whole being up. It's a process that requires you to dream big and listen within, rather than to all those people around you - or your mind.

Deciphering between YOUR truth and other people's opinions, especially when it comes to influencers in your life, such as family, friends, social media, coaches etc can be one of the hardest things to do — it's very similar to distinguishing between the heart and the mind.

It's also about knowing how to manifest, and your mindset plays a huge role in this. There is no point in putting anything out there that you deep down don't believe you could be, do or have. It needs to be something you want to do with ALL of your being, that excites you — your body, mind and spirit at the same time — and that lights you up.

A lot of people make the mistake of going for something that they THINK they believe in and want, but really, it's what someone else wants for them or what they think is EXPECTED of them. This can only ever lead to an unfulfilled, uninspired life that leads to emptiness, a lack of fulfilment and joy, anxiety, depression, even numbness, possibly addictions, mood swings... in short: all but your Limitless Potential and an extraordinary life!

So you can see just how important it is to know what truly lights YOU up.

Once you've established what it is you truly want, and what it is that sets your soul on fire, or at least creates butterflies of excitement in your belly, the next question is: "How do I get there?"

This question, in most cases, does not have a straightforward answer. However, and this might sound outrageous to you; that's irrelevant.

To create your life on your own terms in the magical way you'd like to live it and that resonates with your being, you mainly need to become it. It's not so much the doing all alone that creates it, but really the blend of doing and being.

Yes, strategy is super important. It sets the framework and gives you clarity to know exactly what you need to do at any given point in time to get to your desired outcome. However, there is never just one single way to get you to where you want to be. There is no single right or wrong way. It needs to be in ALIGNMENT with who you are.

There is also no need to make major life changes, purchase another course you won't take action on or anything like that. Of course, that's all nice! However, one of the most important keys to changing your reality and creating what you truly want is shifting your mindset, clearing your subconscious baggage that might be blocking you from getting to where you want to get (and way further), plus understanding how the universe works. That way you can tap into flow and BEING the version of you that lives your dreams. This will enable you to use the universal law of magnetism for your own benefit.

The other part is taking aligned and inspired ACTION.

These components will determine how much you're going to allow yourself to tap into abundance, success, fulfilment and full expression of your true potential. Furthermore, they'll allow you to live your dreams which simultaneously enable you to make the biggest positive impact possible.

Key Takeaways:

- You need to know what you want and truly desire first, in order to be able to take the brakes off, so you can create the life you want to be living and ignite your true potential.

- Having goals that you THINK you want to achieve or others expect of you, will lead to an unfulfilled, uninspired life that leads to emptiness, a lack of fulfilment and joy, anxiety, depression, even numbness, possibly addictions, mood swings...in short: all but your Limitless Potential and an extraordinary life!

- It's about FEELING it in your body and letting yourself "go there" without limitation of possibilities. You mainly need to become the version of you who lives your desires already.

PART 3

THE NEXT LEVEL

MANIFESTATION

I'm now going to share a process with you through which I've manifested a lot of my dreams over the years, including a free car within 5 minutes! It's a sure-fire way to gain clarity of your big vision really fast – if you allow yourself to dream big – and make it happen, even when you might not know all the steps to get there yet!

First, I will run you through an easy and fun 6-step process that will help you refine what you really want. Follow the steps and let yourself feel inspired, as your vision takes on a clear shape. I highly recommend checking out these steps even if you are already very clear on your goals and strategy. See it as a way to test the strength of your alignment with them, which will determine your results.

Depending on where you are currently, you'll be able to find a new or increased enthusiasm as you get more in touch with your dreams and inspirations. The process will allow you to get crystal clear about what you want your future to look like and transform these dreams into your new reality!

How much you'll be able to do this is solely limited by your own imagination and willingness to lift the cage of limitation off your own mind. If you at the same time tap into your Limitless Potential —well, then there are really no limits at all!

No matter what background you come from, in the end, it doesn't matter! On the contrary, what truly matters is your attitude and your commitment to change. It's about you believing in yourself; this will make or break it.

I lived all the dreams that I had before I turned 30. What I wanted was to study what I loved, work in my field and be passionate about what I did, travel the world and have two kids before 30. Well, I'm happy (and proud!) to say that I did all of the above and more!

During all those years I, most often, found myself having chats with friends, customers in the local cafes, and later clients, who all had one thing in common: They felt stuck. But they had dreams. I intuitively started coaching them towards their dreams and I saw stuff happening. It still gives me a tingly feeling when someone steps into themselves, acknowledges their dreams and they realise that they are free to go for them! It makes my heart sing when someone becomes aware of the unique gifts that they bring into this world and strive towards living and sharing them! I absolutely love it when they start making their dreams come true, follow their heart and live a thriving life!

When people remain stuck this shows up as them having physical pains, depression and lack of money or freedom. Since I'm so passionate about helping people overcome the feeling of being stuck, which is so common in this World we live in, I want to share the following process with you. So that we can change the world together — one heart at a time.

I want to share this process because it works.

I share it, because I want to see you live your dreams too and doing so isn't rocket science. In fact, there is a lot of stuff out there these days about "manifesting", "creating your reality" and "The Law of Attraction". When The Secret by Rhonda Byrne came out in 2006, I thought: "Oh wow, finally it's out there" and people who would have never believed me and what I was doing instinctively started to talk about it and live it too. I was so happy to see this truth coming out via different channels, written by authors from all walks of life for people from all walks of life. There are books, videos, courses, you name it - all out there... But are you living it? Are you implementing it?

If the theory of manifestation or "creating your reality" still hasn't hit home for you and you find that although you've been reading and hearing so much about it, it still doesn't seem to happen for you, you might have simply overseen one of the steps to take.

This brings me to the first step. Before you can start applying its laws you first need to understand how the universe works. I find that this step represents the foundation of manifestation and dream creation, as it prepares you for all that's to come. Without having insight into how things work, we can't expect the universe to work in our favour.

You wouldn't want to attempt to fix a car without knowing anything about the engine. I guess it would take a lot of courage and it might work, but it would involve a lot of luck and not necessarily bring the outcome you were hoping for.

"There is a thinking power from which all things are created, and which, in its original state, permeates, penetrates, and fills the interspaces of the universe." Wallace D. Wattles.

A thought in this substance produces the very thing that's imagined by that thought. This means that you can "image-in" your thought, and you can cause what you think to be created in reality. This can be something positive or negative and solely depends on your choice.

There is an ancient North American story of an elder talking to a boy. He tells him of the two wolves that live within one man. One is the one of love, hope and joy. It's the wolf of truthfulness, honesty and loyalty. The other one is the one of anger, fear and hate. The boy asks the elder which one survives and gets to live. The elder replies: *"The one you feed."*

Your subconscious will always look for a target, so if your thoughts are owned by worry and limiting beliefs, it's called "negative goal setting" as in the absence of dreams and goals. In fact, your subconscious will automatically select your dominant thought.

According to Brian Mayne, you simply need to *"set a goal for what you want, build your belief that you will achieve it, and your intuitions will flow to show you the way."* Some people refer to this as being in the flow. Your experiences reflect your positive mindset back to you.

This is what's been happening to me since I learned that you can go for your dreams, which I was taught by my mum. I was little. I had a focus. I was driven to live my dreams and visions. I was determined to make them come true. Life is for living and is not to be wasted on hoping for things to be different or on being unhappy. If you're not happy, change it. That's what I've always thought.

Of course, things get more and more complicated as you grow older, and with a family, for example, there are more responsibilities and different needs to take care of. However, if you do have a dream and take baby steps towards it, it'll come true. As with the commitment that you make, the universe will come and help you. You'll see it in the flow you get to experience, the helpful people who will inevitably cross paths with you and the doors that unexpectedly open where you before would have never seen one.

In order to get into this flow and create your dreams, you'll need to follow these four principles:

1) Creativity

Get out of the rational, acquisitive, solution oriented left brain which governs the right side of our bodies and the masculine energies. Pass over to the right brain, which supplies the left half of our body and houses our CREATIVE mind. This includes art, flow, ideas, expression, breaking out of the box and making magic happen. In order for you to do this, go to a place that's inspiring to you — most often this is in nature — or if you're bound to home or city life, inspire or surround yourself with great artwork, relaxing music etc. Think of stuff that expands you, like a great outlook over the ocean or whatever makes your heart sing.

2) Clarity

You need to form a clear mental picture of what you REALLY want. We'll get to this in a moment.

3) Imagination

Once you've gotten crystal clear on what you want, you need to hold its exact picture in your IMAGINATION — with the fixed purpose of achieving what you want with an unwavering faith and the expectation that you will indeed get what you really want. That means you'll need to stay positive, overcome obstacles, release old self-sabotage patterns and believe what you IMAGE-IN (imagine) is real. To super-charge this step, imagine your desired outcome is already here, it's already done. The more you can FEEL it in your body to be true already, the easier it will be to create it.

4) Action

In order for you to receive what you really want when the opportunity arises, you need to take aligned action. Most visionary leaders and business owners I had the pleasure to work with up till now know how to take action quite well.

However, is it ALIGNED and inspired action? Most often not. If you work under pressure, due to obligations and the "musts" and "shoulds" (in other words Dogma) or try to do everything at once, chances are that you won't be in flow and not in the right vibe to attract your desired outcomes to you.

What does 'vibe' or 'vibration' mean?

A vibration is, when you think a thought and it feels a certain way, or you say a word and it feels a certain way, or you feel an emotion and it feels a certain way. Every thought, word, energy, literally everything has a vibration. It has a frequency. And a frequency will attract more of the same frequency

If someone says to you, *"I love you"* from a place of pure, unconditional love from their heart, then you feel the vibe of love. Everything has a vibration. And we can think thoughts, say words and feel feelings to bring vibrations into our body, to bring vibrations into our energetic space, and therefore into our field.

The more you imagine what you dream of to be real and the more action you take towards this dream, the more excited you feel and the more into flow you get.

We attract people, situations and experiences into our life all the time. We can only attract those with the same frequency as ourselves. So if you want to create wealth, freedom and abundance on all levels, we need to hold the frequency that matches that. There's no wonder why there are so many people that want to create wealth, but don't seem to get there. Most people have a low deserving energy from deep underlying shame, guilt or grief trapped in their body and therefore can't make it happen. If we carry shame, guilt and dogma in ourselves, the mass limitations and restrictions and pressure, we can't attract freedom and abundance vibes. It's just not possible.

Same goes for when we attract our soulmate. It happens once you actually love yourself deeper. Then all the rest disappears; all limitations, the frequency rises, and you attract the match.

In order to attract what you want to attract into your field, you need to up your consciousness and wealth consciousness levels. Therefore, you want to clear the baggage that's holding you back and keeping you stuck and attached, so you can rise and choose to up your vibe, your frequency, and therefore attract all the goodness in.

It's very straightforward. Once you're in the flow, and you keep at it, you're on the road to success!

What is success?

According to Earl Nightingale it's "the progressive realisation of personal worthy goals or ideals".

My greatest passion is assisting others to step into their Limitless Potential and achieving success with it, i.e., achieving their aligned goals. Since I was a little girl, I always found it super exciting tapping into someone's dreams and true desires and after supporting and coaching them and getting closer to them, seeing them actually living them! It sends shivers down my spine for someone to ignite and live their dreams, truth and potential.

What are goals?

Goals are dreams with a time frame.

If you want to achieve success and manifest your dreams into reality, you need to turn them into goals first. Now is the time for fresh goals to be written up and focused on, as this is another one of the secrets of success — Do it NOW!

The strangest secret of succeeding in manifesting your dreams is that you become what you visualise yourself to be.

You might know the movie *What the Bleep Do We Know*. In it, the lady looks into the mirror and sees herself exactly the way she thinks she looks. Her thoughts and visualisations are so powerful that she ends up looking exactly like them. Therefore, if you want to lose weight, but constantly focus on the extra flab, that might not even be very obvious to anyone else, you will make that extra flab appear for all others too!

If you want to use this universal rule, your visualisation needs to be really YOUR truth.

You can visualise all you want, but if that picture isn't really what you want it probably won't come true for you. It needs to be in complete alignment with you and who you are.

So the first step in the dream-goal-setting process is discovering what you really want. Yes, what YOU really want!

Overall, there are six simple steps you can use to discover (and manifest) what it is that you really want so that you can then make it all happen, which are described on the following pages.

No more "I don't really know what I want" after that!

Key Takeaways:

- According to Universal Law, a thought produces the very thing that's imagined by that thought. This means that you can "image-in" your thought, and you can cause what you think to be created in reality.

- Your subconscious will always look for a target, so if your thoughts are owned by worry and limiting beliefs, it's called "negative goal setting" as in the absence of dreams and goals. In fact, your subconscious will automatically select your dominant thought. It can be as simple as *"set a goal for what you want, build your belief that you will achieve it, and your intuitions will flow to show you the way."*

- How much you'll be able to manifest your dreams and vision is solely limited by your own imagination and willingness to lift the cage of limitation off your own mind.

CREATING SPACE FOR WHAT YOU WANT

First, you'll need to make space for what you want. This is particularly relevant if you've been trying hard to move forward, take the right steps and do the right things, but all you've been hearing and seeing is crickets.

Why is that?

Because you need to shift the old first. This can be in the form of...

- Decluttering your house, your space, your email inbox or your wallet
- Sorting out your old mindset and beliefs
- Ending relationships that have become toxic or misaligned
- Changing your body weight, if you don't feel good about it. Body fat cells store toxins; old toxins which have previously entered our life as environmental toxins, negative thoughts, yucky emotions, etc. You get the picture.

This extra weight you carry, in the form of...

- Dense or trapped emotions that can flare up as frustration, anger, sabotage, feeling sluggish or tired, to name a few
- Too much stuff in your house that doesn't give you joy
- Broken things that make you feel shabby or poor
- Misaligned relationships, overstepped boundaries, toxic interactions and dynamics
- Clutter that annoys you when you look at it, or that clouds your mind as you think of all the things you still need to do, sort, etc.

...These ultimately leave you feeling low, right?

These create a contracting feeling within, as you feel guilty, ashamed or negative about yourself for not having sorted/ done/ let go of it yet. This low feeling and contraction then create an extreme contrast to the expansion, lightness and happiness that your dream vision makes you feel.

It's a vibrational mismatch and called cognitive dissonance.

"Cognitive dissonance refers to a situation involving conflicting attitudes, beliefs or behaviours. This produces a feeling of discomfort, leading to an alteration in one of the attitudes, beliefs or behaviours to reduce the discomfort and restore balance, etc."[4]

It tells you that what is in your conscious mind might not be matching your subconscious mind. You can tell yourself to be positive and grateful all you want, or that you really want a certain outcome. However, if your body, as a representation of your subconscious, is holding a different belief or feeling, it's not authentic, and that will make manifesting your dreams really hard. Therefore, if you want to create an abundant life and business, not just monetary, but also in your relationships, feeling amazing and fulfilled, and you find it's not happening on all levels, then there is definitely something going on internally that will keep you trapped and lower your deserving levels. This is very, very common.

Have you ever experienced this?

Most likely. And the advice is to simply address it.

So let me recap, UNLESS you've...

- Dealt with your stories and beliefs
- Cleared your stuff
- And created SPACE for the new...

...you won't be able to RECEIVE what you're putting out there for.

---

[4] Saul Mcleod, PhD; Simply Psychology: What is Cognitive Dissonance? Definition and Examples; https://www.simplypsychology.org/cognitive-dissonance.html.

Unless you step up and make space in your life/body/consciousness/home/heart/mind — meaning you...

- Declutter the old that doesn't serve you any longer
- Free yourself of old trapped emotions, stories and beliefs
- And rewire your brain to positivity and expansion...

...you won't be able to RECEIVE what you're putting out there for.

The old version of you can't attract what you want. The old version of you with the old thoughts, stories, beliefs, emotions and messiness cluttering your inner and outer spaces won't be able to create your next level, as otherwise you would have done so a long time ago already.

Believe me, it will feel immensely liberating letting go and clearing out!

Plus, it really works.

A tip for this process is to feel into each item (this applies to stuff in your house or office, foods and thoughts alike) and check whether it makes you feel INspired or EXpired. Doing this process on all levels will lead to quantum leaping. It clearly states to the universe what you're done with and don't accept in your life anymore. It clearly indicates what gives you joy and want more of, and it provides space for more of what you desire to come into your life. Therefore, I highly recommend going and focusing more on what makes you feel good and on "Bliss hunting", as I like to call it, and less on problem-solving. Allow yourself to make space for this bliss, and radically say no to what doesn't serve you. It's quite simple really, but a game changer.

Key Takeaways:

- To create what you want or attract it into your life (no matter if material, feeling, love etc), you need to make space and shift and let go of the old first.

- Cognitive dissonance is extra weight in form of baggage, broken things, misalignment and clutter that create a contracting feeling within, as you feel guilty, ashamed or negative about yourself for not having sorted/ done/let go of it yet. This low feeling and contraction then create an extreme contrast to the expansion, lightness and happiness that your dream vision makes you feel and won't let you create it.

- The old version of you can't attract what you want. You need to become the version of you who will be, do or have what you desire, so you can attract it to you.

DREAM - GOAL CREATION

Now, it is time to get crystal clear on what it is that YOU truly want, as you can try and manifest all sorts of stuff, but if it's not what YOU really desire then it probably won't come true, or if it does, it won't feel fulfilling for you. Let's look at the 6 steps to create your dream goals now:

Step 1: Write up a crazy list of dreams
The best way to discover this is to imagine all the dreams you have for yourself first. Take a piece of paper, turn it so you're holding it horizontally and put your name and the date on the top. Then use the following headers, or some that are equally meaningful for you, and place them next to each other. These are going to be the headers for your roughly 10 columns.

Draw up headings under:

1. Personal
2. Financial
3. Career
4. Family/Social
5. Physical
6. Spiritual
7. Mental
8. Creative
9. Environmental
10. Material
11. Travel
12. Emotions
13. Hobbies

Add more if you'd like. Really, you can choose whatever is important for you right now. These are just commonly used header examples.

Then go on a crazy dream list brainstorm.

Come up with as many dreams on this list as you can, so 10–100 dreams under each header would be a great start. List anything that you've ever wanted or can imagine for yourself, no matter how ridiculous or how impossible it may seem. It's not important what you are writing down. This step is just part of the process; it's opening up your imagination to help you find out what you really truly want.

Don't question the validity of what's coming up. Just write your dreams down, the more the better. Don't worry thinking about whether they are logical, realistic or achievable from where you are at right now. Remember, these are supposed to be your dreams and, in our dreams, anything is possible!

So if you always wanted to live in a castle, write that down. If you'd like to have a fit and healthy body, the love of your life, a year to travel wherever you want... Write it down!

And remember: Limitations are a creation of the mind!

Step 2: Add a time frame
Go through all of your 10 to 100 dreams per category and sort them into three groups based on their time frames. This is to differentiate between those things you'd like to have happen right now and those that you know will take a bit longer. This part of the exercise will require you to be a bit more realistic. For example, if you'd love to be a piano player, you can, by working on it, definitely attain this within 1–2 years. If you're dreaming about running a multimillion-dollar business or owning a castle but you don't have those millions in the bank yet, you might just want to give yourself a bit more time. I'd recommend marking your individual dreams with the following letters:

A   for short-term goals (i.e. attainable within the next 3 months -1 year)
B   for medium-term goals (i.e. attainable within 2 -3 years)
C   for long-term goals (i.e. attainable in 5 + years)

Now your dreams have been transformed into goals, as you have put time frames on them!

Step 3: Ask yourself, does it excite you?

This next exercise is where it gets interesting: Now sort out the three most relevant or exciting goals for you in each of those three time frames.

Now it's all starting to happen... Your dreams at this moment are starting the process of manifestation!

Overcome your fear of success...if what you have written expands and excites you deeply within, when you imagine it being true already... CIRCLE IT!

Are you excited when you think about it? Does it make you feel uplifted? Then circle it, highlight it. However, if you just THOUGHT you wanted it, but you FEEL rather tired, overwhelmed, pressured and contracted when you think about it, then it is not a dream-goal of yours, it's something you THINK you should be wanting, but it's actually someone else's dream. So simply go by what makes YOU feel really excited, tingly, happy, open, and expanded deep inside.

Step 4: Focus on what's most exciting!

Now choose the most important or exciting one of your short, medium and long-term goals. This can sometimes be the trickiest part of the whole process. You want it all and certainly don't just want to settle for one alone? Rest assured, you won't have to!

By picking one goal for each time frame, you just narrow down your vision to be more focused. Simply circle your choice. By focusing on one dream-goal for each time frame, you won't have to dismiss or decide against any of your other goals. No, on the contrary; it's very likely that all the other 'side goals' will become reality too, as you will allow space for them to happen. It's also always easier and more powerful to visualise one thing at a time, as opposed to a gazillion things at once.

It's like when you're planning on doing too many things in one day—all that ends up happening is that you're starting to feel edgy, overwhelmed and stressed. You're running around like crazy, but in the end, you don't accomplish a single thing. Instead, you'll feel like you grazed over tons of stuff and feel fried.

If you instead set yourself one main focus for the day, it's very likely you're going to get it done. Moreover, you'll feel amazing, clear and inspired on top!

It's the same for visualisations. Focus, and you'll get somewhere — fast!

Pick the most exciting goal for each:

A) Short-term goals
B) Medium-term goals
C) Long-term goals

Once you've got your 3 goals for your short-term, medium and long-term goals clarified, do a cross check. Ask yourself the following questions and be really honest and authentic with yourself when answering them:

Is your choice...

- Realisable?
- Practical within the time frame?
- Your goal (as opposed to someone else's ideal for you)?
- Does your choice excite your imagination??

The last two questions can be easily answered by listening within: does the thought of it EXPAND you? Or does it CONTRACT you with worry, fear or tension in the tummy area?

Once you're clear on those answers, write down your choice of one of each of your short, medium and long-term goals as you see them in the present tense. So instead of writing *"I will"*, you'll put *"I am"*. You can even say *"I have"* in past tense. Do all this in a long imaginative sentence, just the way you see your goal in your mind's eye. The more specific and vivid, the better.

Can you feel it? Can you sense what it will look, sound, smell and feel like? The more emotionally loaded you can make the visualisation, the more real it becomes and the more easily you'll manifest your goal into reality.

Step 5: Visualise and take aligned action
If you're looking for alignment, fulfilment, health, vitality and making a massive positive impact, whilst making a lot of money at the same time,

then you need a BALANCED approach of BEing and DOing. It will depend on the right balance here:

- If you naturally dream and visualise a lot, journal and are generally good at 'being', you will need to step into ACTION more. Note: This needs to be ALIGNED action, NOT spinning the wheels.
- If you're great at taking action and getting tasks done, DO a lot and never stop, you will need to learn how to BE more. Being means knowing how to get yourself into an inspired state that feels relaxed and receptive.

Visualisation is super important in manifesting your dreams and desires.

You can do it like this:

After writing down the sentences in the previous step, place that sheet of paper with your three main goals where you can see it and remind yourself of it every day. For example, you can pin it up on the wall next to the toilet. The fridge door or dashboard of your car are some other good spots. Some mentors, such as Denise Duffield Thomas from the Lucky Bitch Bootcamp, suggest that you change all your passwords to your new and highest goal. She calls this process "Goal Spreading". You can also make a vision board, screensavers or create an online version of your vision board, which can grow and change with your developing vision. Again, your limitations are simply a creation of your mind!

This ongoing visualisation process is particularly important for Specific Manifestors in Human Design. If you're not sure which one you are or what Human Design is, look up your free chart online at *myhumandesign.com* (all you need is your birth date, place and the exact time of your birth). Then look for the four arrows in the top of your chart. If the bottom arrow from the top on the right side is pointing to the left, you're a Specific Manifestor. If it's pointing to the right, you're a Non-specific Manifestor. This means you'll mainly need to FEEL into your desired outcome as if it's already here.

You really need to visualise, no matter if that means SEEING your goals and vision or FEELING it to be true already every day, as you need to retrain your brain to believe your new reality. The key here is to visualise your desires as if they've already happened. Much like a muscle that needs consistent use to stay strong, your brain needs to practise this new way of thinking until it becomes a new habit.

Now we come to the action part of this step. You can visualise all you want, but if you don't follow this up with real ACTION then it's going to stay a dream forever.

Therefore, I ask you to write down your three main goals as headers now. Then add in the next action steps that you'll need to take to get there.

If you're dreaming of becoming a well-known speaker, you can put down 1) Create a media one sheet - 2) Apply for podcasts and speaking gigs - 3) Reach out to other influencers.

Break your dream down into actionable baby steps and then move towards your main goal. The more detailed and clear the better, as it's going to help you execute them.

Once you've done that, you've got your action plan ready. Now it's up to you to follow your own action steps.

The keys here are; focus, consistency and vibrational alignment. Keep holding the feeling, even when there's no evidence that it's going to happen. Continue to vibrate with the outcome that you want, even when there's no reason to believe that it can occur.

You need to be in a high vibe state to show the universe you're ready and matching what you want the outcome to be, as like attracts like.

An important point to note here is that it's not enough to pretend to be happy and fake a high vibe state—as that's simply not going to work. So, if you're not FEELING it, it's ok. Simply clear your charge rather than suppressing how you're actually feeling, as that will only backfire. It's all about acknowledgment of those parts so they can be let go of.

Step 6: Stay on Track
This step is all about learning the 'rules' around manifestation and getting a few hints around what to do and what to avoid.

Number 1: You create your reality.

Number 2: Remind yourself of your goals - all the time.

Number 3: Focus, focus, focus.

Number 4: Remember to take inspired action, in order for 'it' to come.

Number 5: Keep envisioning 'it' to be here already.

Number 6: Remember, like attracts like.

Number 7: Stop putting your own needs last.

Number 8: BE and DO now what you want to HAVE later.

You need to be exactly those things now that you want to do or feel once you're "there", so you can create the "there" in the now and live how you want to live already.

This part of the process gets referred to as "future pacing".

You can take a selfie video and pretend you're talking to yourself from a point 5+ years in the future, looking back. You can rave about how life looks and feels now that you've achieved and are living all your dreams. Show and feel how excited and proud you feel for having gotten there and about how amazing it feels.

The more you can make yourself FEEL it, the more likely it is that you'll be seeing it come to fruition really fast.

This is how I made all of my travel, round the world trips, kids, cars, house, etc happen; I IMAGED (and of course ACTIONED) them IN. This is a crucial part.

You'll need to act with the people and things in your present life and work towards your goal. Follow the clues and leads that come your way and act upon them. Again, when you do this you'll be in the flow: All of a sudden, the right people and situations come into your life. One step leads to the next.

Coincidence? Most definitely not! It's your creation!

The keys to staying on track are:

1) Consistent Action
Remember it's ok to have those off days, or days needed to nurture and nourish, but overall, it's imperative to stay laser focused.

When people ask me how I can consistently have the energy to show up for all that I do, my answer is: Get clear on your "Big Why" and you'll never have to worry about commitment, energy and motivation again. If you connect with the higher reason of WHY you want your dreams to become a reality, and the answer is a balance between altruistic, serving others and the world, and narcissistic, self-serving reasons, you have a strong foundation. In order to get clear on your WHY, it helps to continuously ask yourself, "And what will that give them/me?" until you end up at the highest reason of all.

If we truly connect with our businesses, services, products and the outcomes and ripple effects they are creating, we can feel way more easily into their value. We can stand strong and proud knowing that what we love doing is way bigger than us and that we need to show up, no matter how small and insignificant we can feel at times. We are not powerless and by doing our bit, no matter how small, we can create a ripple effect into the world.

Knowing your Big Why will give you a constant reminder of why you do what you do and of its higher purpose and meaning, and this will result in you having tons of energy, passion and enthusiasm which you won't be able to help yourself putting into consistent action as you're so inspired.

2) Mindset
It's totally normal to have all sorts of stuff coming up that tries to get you off the track that leads to your purpose and dreams (that's if they're big enough). I'll be going into this soon, in my next chapter, *Resistance*. Keep working on these negative beliefs, patterns and forms of resistance and try to not let them lead you astray!

This requires a fine balance between processing and integrating. In other words, acknowledging what's coming up and shifting it, whilst having firm boundaries allowing you to march straight past these signposts of resistance that are trying to tell you that turning around will be the best and safest solution ever.

Therefore, keep clearing. If you don't know how to do so, journal, make notes, do regular brain-dumps, shadow flipping and process your life beyond to-do lists. Take moments to just sit and reflect and let your thoughts drift without guiding them. Keep shifting your perception to stay inspired and move forward.

In short, do anything you need for your brain to stay calm, clear and focused and for your life to be decluttered and organised. Be in your centre and body. Remember that only where there is space and receptivity, can new ideas develop, and dreams can become reality. Only if there is space that matches the frequency of what you want, can abundance come on all levels.

3) Commitment

Usually keeping an eye on your grand vision and Big Why is enough to keep you committed as it's your purpose to share your gift with the world, but sometimes you might need a reminder. Use the power of the mind to create the life you're dreaming of. Work with mind-boards, beautiful notes that you can pin to the wall, pictures (if you are a visual person), and set yourself some daily goals you want to achieve. Write and rewrite your big vision and goals all the time, but what I mean here is make sure you break it down.

Make a list of 3 top goals (smaller tangible steps towards your big goals and visions) every single day or week, depending on how busy you are and how big your "bite-sized steps" are. Once you've achieved them, tick them off. That way you fill yourself with gratitude for how far you've come. A healthy sense of pride and achievement at the end of each day will in turn build your self-esteem, help you believe in yourself and get you a few steps closer to your big vision and dreams. This forms a positive, self-perpetuating cycle which will reinforce your overall commitment and keep you going with even more energy than before.

Key Takeaways:

- Get crystal clear on what it is that YOU truly want, as you can try and manifest all sorts of stuff, but if it's not what you really desire then it probably won't come true, or if it does, it won't feel fulfilling for you.

- If you're looking for alignment, fulfilment, health, vitality and making a massive positive impact, whilst making a lot of money at the same time, then you need a BALANCED approach of BEing and DOing. It will depend on the right balance.

- The keys to staying on track are:
Consistent Action – Mindset – Commitment.

RESISTANCE

"In physics, resistance is a measure of the tendency of a material to resist the flow of an electrical current. (...)"[5]

In other words, resistance is a measure of the tendency to struggle against you moving forward. When we expand beyond what's known to us (our comfort zone), our subconscious resistance patterns kick in. Resistance is a form of keeping us in check so to speak, as our subconscious vehemently wants to "protect" us from exploring what else is out there.

It might cause fatigue, yawning, general tiredness, listlessness, vagueness, denial etc.

Our comfort zone feels safe - no matter if it's totally detrimental to our (mental) health and wellbeing or not, it simply feels safe as it's known and familiar. Anything out of our comfort zone appears scary and threatening to our ego. Therefore, it pulls us back and keeps us small.

I like to explain resistance with the analogy of an elastic band.

Imagine standing in the middle of a circular rug with a pole in its centre. Your legs are tied to the pole with an elastic band. Now you are taking a few steps away from the pole, until you eventually reach the edge of the rug.

As you step out of your Comfort Zone and expand into your Learning Zone, the elastic band around the pole in the centre of your Comfort Zone and your legs stretches. Once you hit "Danger Zone" (too far away from the centre of your Comfort Zone), it will fling you back to where you were before (or even further back).

---

[5] Wisegeek. 2019. In Physics, what is Resistance?

What is Resistance?

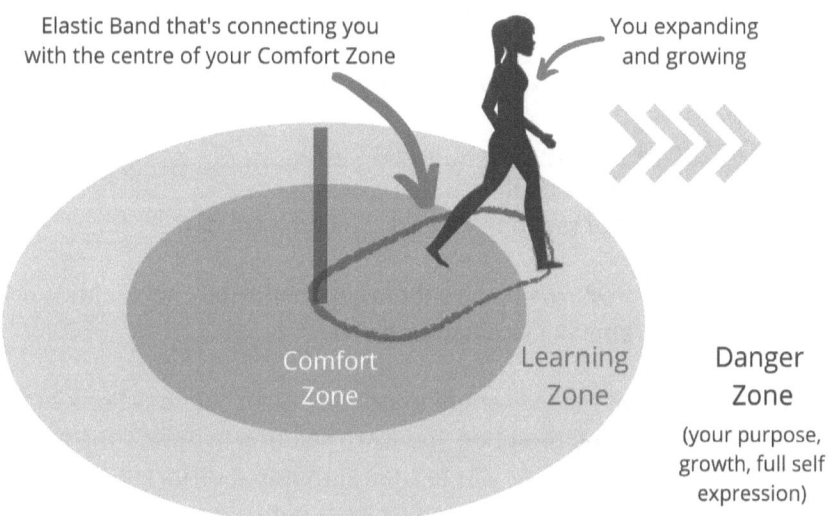

Elastic Band that's connecting you with the centre of your Comfort Zone

You expanding and growing

Comfort Zone

Learning Zone

Danger Zone

(your purpose, growth, full self expression)

As you step out of your Comfort Zone and expand into your Learning Zone, the elastic band around the pole in the centre of your Comfort Zone and your legs stretches. Once you hit "Danger Zone"; you're too far away from the centre of your Comfort Zone, it will fling you back to where you were before (or even further back).

© Sand Mew

In that moment the elastic band has reached its maximum elasticity and flings you right back to the centre of your comfort zone, or maybe even further back. That's why we can be quite in the flow sometimes and then all of a sudden find ourselves in an old, stuck state again. Maybe you've asked yourself before: *"How did I manage to end up back here again?? What did I do wrong??"*

Instead, we should really be asking ourselves: *"What did I do so right in order to end up back here again?"*

Whatever it was, it has challenged all our old beliefs of how things are so much that our subconscious framework, I like to refer to this as our "cage", freaked out. In fact, it freaked out so much that it flung us straight back into the old familiar struggle.

This subconscious fear isn't true, it simply indicates that what lies in the "danger zone" exceeds our expectation, level of comfort or familiarity. Therefore, the expanded thought or state of being appears very unsettling and unsafe to our subconsciousness, which will now try to hold us back with all its might.

This may come in the form of negative self-talk:

- "Oh, I knew it wasn't going to work out."
- "I knew I couldn't do it."
- "It was crazy of me to think that it could work out."

Furthermore, it often shows up as sabotaging behaviour, accidents, hurting yourself, or even drama in life all around you.

Sound familiar? All of these examples happen in your subconscious' attempt to convince you that the direction you were heading in wasn't the right one in the first place, in order for you to then turn into a different direction (or not at all) and try again from scratch (or best not try at all and stay in your old comfort zone instead). Until, one day, you hit the same level of stretch and start all over again.

Our negative self-beliefs and patterns of resistance can hold us back tremendously. We all have conscious and subconscious patterns that are keeping us in check.

Our negative self-beliefs, maps, cognitive dissonance, trapped emotions, conditioning and more influence our thinking and mindset.

There are 7 main forms of resistance that come up for all of us.

They hold us back from living our Limitless Potential. These patterns creep up unnoticed. They limit us and hold us back from shining. They block us from fully embodying ourselves, feeling clear and energised.

It's so easy to get stuck and lose that level of inner connection. We all have stuff coming up at times. It's a matter of paying attention to and familiarising yourself with your patterns of resistance, so you can work on them - and recognise where you're at in the first place.

Despite our best efforts, sometimes it's necessary to get a professional outside perspective from a coach, mentor and/or clearing practitioner, somebody who can hold a bigger container for you to expand into.

To keep going with much more ease and speed yourself, learn *Take The Brakes Off™ - Self Clearing*, to shift these constructs of limitations and free yourself of them within a matter of minutes.

However, even if you don't have any of these tools and skills yet, what I'm about to share with you is pivotal and will lay the foundations for you to be able to navigate what comes up with so much more ease and certainty.

Even just being aware of what is playing out and being able to recognise your patterns and adjust your course accordingly, will empower you to take your life back into your own hands. Rather than getting hijacked like a leaf in the wind and being at the mercy of your subconscious patterns trying to protect you from harm, you'll be able to take your power back.

When we strive to reach new goals or live our purpose, there seems to be all sorts of crazy stuff that comes up - often out of nowhere - and it holds us back.

When I first came across this concept many years ago, it had been on my list for years to write my first online mentoring program. I knew how beneficial it was going to be for so many. However, subconsciously, I had a ton of stuff coming up around visibility and sharing my message, and as I was focusing on my end goal (to get it all written), I had pretty much all forms of resistance under the sun thrown my way, including a fire behind my house!! At that time, I hadn't discovered the power of self-clearing yet and therefore couldn't do all that much myself, except regularly booking myself into clearing sessions with another practitioner, and repeating positive affirmations.

Resistance / sabotage is normal and definitely NOT a conscious choice or your fault. It's the way we deal with it and if we give it the power to take over or not, that really matters.

The way I could tell that this was sabotage playing out, rather than the universe telling me that it wasn't meant to be, as it did in other instances, was by me commanding sabotage to "step aside, step aside now" and fully activating my conscious presence and spirit back in my body again. As soon as I did this, the fog, doubt or whatever sensations I had would shift, and I was able to refocus with new-found clarity and determination in regards to my vision. This showed me that I was on the right track, and that it was internally or externally created resistance patterns that were trying to hold me back.

In order to be able to do this, it is imperative to be aware of the 7 main forms of resistance. Without familiarising yourself with these patterns first and your own default ones, you'll have a hard time spotting them amidst the busyness of life. (Believe me, they do a great job at camouflaging themselves!)

Understanding them will help you to not only recognise forms of resistance easier. It will help you navigate them, become more familiar with your own unique forms of resistance and tackle them with the self clearing tools. You'll be able to understand and navigate your own patterns of resistance easier, so you can do the self clearing, so they aren't holding you back so much, or not at all anymore.

The 7 Forms of Resistance

I was first introduced to this concept by my mentor, Nicola Grace 'The Mission Mentor', and they all made so much sense to me.

#1 - Self-Doubt

Do you keep telling yourself that your dreams are too big and ask yourself, "Who am I to think that I can do this?!"

Self-doubt is one of the main forms of resistance. It's a form of resistance to expressing who you are and ultimately being a bigger version of who you were before. It shows up as worthiness issues, holding yourself back because of fear of greatness and not letting yourself be seen for who you are.

It might show up in one of the following ways. You might ...

- Keep telling yourself that you can't do something — and therefore keep proving to yourself that you truly can't, by constantly setting yourself up for failure.
- Feel deep down that you don't deserve it. That you must work hard in order to achieve it and that things don't drop from the sky.
- Think you're not qualified enough to take the next steps. Not good enough. Not authoritative enough. You might not feel it's perfect enough. Not yet. So you hold back.

You doubt, you worry, you think. And worse: You stop. Self-doubt freezes you in your tracks. It cripples you, and it eats you.

Did you know that some psychologists say that more than 90% of self-talk is negative? A large amount of our time gets spent dealing with self-doubt. Some people even spend very prolonged times of their lives with this limiting and destructive feeling.

When trying something different, have you ever thought of how much time you spend doubting your abilities? Did you realise that self-doubt is the biggest time waster?

In the moment when self-doubt strikes, we tend to spontaneously mix our inner knowing with controlling thought patterns.

Who hasn't heard someone in their life who said, "So you think you're special, do you?" or "Why do you think you're different to everybody else?"

We compare ourselves to others, feel deflated, insecure and generally not good/far enough/fast enough to get the job done. So we hold back and the sabotage pattern wins, that's trying to keep us small and in our comfort zone.

This sabotage pattern is strong, so watch out. Remember it's trying to "protect" you from exploring what else is out there. It pulls you back and keeps you small with the intention of shielding you from pain. However, this pattern isn't aware that it'll cause you even more pain by making you miss out on the experience of growing and becoming a more empowered, integrated and expanded human being.

In order to combat self-doubt, flip the story and instead tell yourself, *"I am worthy of living my dream. If I live my passions and purpose, I'll lift people up all around me and ultimately inspire change in the world."*

Create a strategy, align your actions, stay in your field of strength, hang out with affirming people, use your network as a "lift as you climb" and track your accomplishments.

Build your confidence by:

- Continuously clearing trapped emotions and beliefs or get a trusted practitioner who can help you to do so
- Coming back to and following your inner truth
- Following your inspirations and dreams
- Developing spiritually, personally and professionally
- Joining social media groups, masterminds and hiring a coach or mentor to support you

Do whatever it takes to stay inspired and keep moving. Whatever you do, just don't stop and give into the doubt, as otherwise you've let sabotage win and the World will miss out on what you've got to share.

#2 - Fear (or Lack of Trust)

Fear, or lack of trust, pops up commonly when the goal to achieve seems to be too big and you feel like it would involve a whole massive life change, i.e. selling up the house or breaking up your relationship. "How could I ever do this?"

Flip the story: "This dream might seem huge, but I choose to break it down into baby steps."

It's never all or nothing. Everything can be broken down into bite-size steps. You will never reach the top of a mountain if you don't start making the first steps at some stage. Break down your dream into baby steps!

You can also establish a power hour, get a study buddy and hire a coach or mentor.

In order to move forward, we really need to become friends with fear and learn how to read and utilise it as a form of compass. Where there is fear, there is room for growth!

Again, this depends on what type of fear is playing out. Is it fluttering and quite high up in your chest, throat or head area? Then it's probably indicating room for growth and an opportunity for expansion.

However, if it's low in the abdomen, screwing deeper down, it's more a sense of foreboding, telling you that something is not right. In that case it's important to take note of and heed the warning.

#3 - Distractions (e.g., procrastination, family dramas, other big stuff or poor time management)

"I don't have the time". This is a big one, as so many of us think we are too busy to achieve yet another thing. Very often time and money are key areas in which people tend to feel stuck and powerless. If your feeling of limitation comes from a lack of time, it all comes down to productivity and where you place your focus.

Have you heard of the 80-20 rule?

80% of things get achieved in 20% of the time.

That leaves the question: What do we actually end up doing with the remainder?

Right! Procrastinate, hang on Facebook, flick between tasks...

Really, we waste time all the time.

When I did the online business program B-School with Marie Forleo many years ago, I thought I was really busy with my little kids, part-time job and seeing clients. However, I felt it was really important for me to do this program. As it was a big investment for us at the time, I wanted to make every cent of it count. I scraped together time and seemingly pulled it out of nowhere. As a result, I managed to gain an extra 20 hours of time to work on the program a week! I was mind blown.

Of course, it's all different if someone is sick or you're simply alone with everything in your family setup. However, even then there are various ways of responding: you can bury your head in the sand and freak out, or you look for help and different ways to deal with the situation.

What can make a world of a difference to feeling stuck in a rut with time? Try the following:

- Be super diligent in tracking what you spend your time on.
- Assess whether all these tasks are aligned with your values and where you want to go. You may ask yourself: Am I doing this task because I truly believe that it's important or because I've been conditioned to THINK it has to be done?
- Get clear on what you'd like to achieve instead and what steps you need to take to get there.
- Let go of tasks that are not in alignment with your needs and truth. An example would be letting people step over your boundaries and over-giving to the point of you feeling drained and exhausted.
- Delegate tasks.
- Choose proper time slots for important activities that you'd like to spend your time on but usually end up sacrificing. Prioritize getting the items on your urgent to-do list *done.*
- Stick to the plan you're now creating instead of doing what you've done in the past.

For every other distraction, name the game!

If you work for yourself, ask yourself, "What would I do if I had a full-time job?"

The distraction is more than likely going to vanish!

#4 - Denial

Are you yawning? Feeling drained? Thinking that you're all of a sudden so tired...?

Did you know that subconscious denial causes inner friction which results in fatigue and exhaustion? Note: this is most often NOT a conscious thought!

Sometimes a part of us doesn't want to see the obvious.

It can express itself in physical ways with body tension and signs and symptoms showing up in a specific area of our body and of course in our headspace. Yawning is a typical first sign of resistance and denial.

"Since you can't see what you can't see, you need to have someone hold the torch at your feet". Get yourself a mentor, trusted friend or colleague, or clearing practitioner, and take full responsibility for yourself and your creations. We all need someone to hold a bigger container for us that we can grow into.

#5 - Amnesia

When this denial is getting bigger and you're not ready to hear certain information yet, what can happen is that you simply forget what was being said.

When the vision of someone's purpose or Limitless Potential challenges the person's comfort zone a lot, it can happen that they simply block out and forget what was being said in the first place — which is why I offer recordings of the sessions with my clients.

This allows them to listen back to it again over time, which in itself can be very powerful. They don't just not forget what was being said, but they'll also be able to hear, extract and integrate more and more goodness of what we covered during our sessions. That way, they can slowly adjust to the expanded vision and transmission (the vibration) which had triggered their subconsciousness into "freak out" mode in the first place.

You can only ever pick up the knowledge, skills and pieces of information that you're ready for at any given time. That's also why we can read certain books over and over again and still always learn something new.

Another solution to avoid the resistance pattern of amnesia is by making notes straight after hearing something extremely expansive about yourself (or having a download'), rather than waiting a few hours or expecting to remember it all after returning to a busy day.

If what you heard or 'downloaded' (and this can easily happen after having a mentoring session) was particularly expansive, you might either not remember what was said OR you won't be able to tap into the feeling or frequency of the expansion later anymore — unless you've got notes or a recording to remind you of it again.

Now, take a look and assess. Have you been in denial and even forgetting the things that you know would get you further? Once you're honest with yourself, start the ball rolling by making the decision that you want more than this. That you're over ignoring stuff. That you'll end this road of denial and blending facts out. You can do so here and now.

Once you've made the decision that you want more because you know that there is way more to life than living in a soup of denial and unhappiness, you've made the first step. It is the biggest one of all, by the way.

Then look within. If you know what to do, start following this inner guidance now. Don't hold back anymore.

If you don't know what to do, how to listen and not get run over by a million voices that seem to freeze you even more, reach out or get yourself a mentor that understands you. You'll achieve your goals faster and stay on track.

Don't get OUT of your comfort zone, EXPAND it instead!

#6 - Aloneness

"I've got to do it all!"

On the entrepreneurial journey that most of us are on, we can get sucked into doing it all and working around the clock for it. This can be quite a lonely road, as it isolates us from community. I had done this for many years, and it was certainly not the easiest way!

When we learn to delegate and make systems, we actually create space to connect and network and make things easier and more fun for everyone — and therefore eliminate aloneness altogether.

It's easy to lose focus, so it really pays off to hire a mentor who keeps you accountable and on track. But also masterminds, study buddies, and meet up groups run by more expanded individuals — a community who you can check in with on a regular basis and who remind you of who you really are — does the trick of helping you stay on track, expand and grow into a bigger version of yourself.

It's good to enjoy a fair share of "me time", to be able to tell where you start and end as an individual, to get solid on who you are and not get swayed by the people around you. However, don't believe your subconscious mind's trick that tells you you're all alone and have to do it all by yourself!

It's important to remember that we can all hold a bigger container for each other. If we were meant to be able to do all the amazing things we can do for others for ourselves too, why would we coexist at all? Why would we have the human need to connect and love? Coming together, exchanging, supporting and growing together brings about an energy and joy that is exponential. Don't deprive yourself of this.

Surround yourself with a high frequency container of friends, a mentor, mastermind or a meet up group. You become like the 4 closest people that you surround yourself with.

If you spend lots of time with people that you feel tired or deflated by, look into what motivates you to spend time with them in the first place. Is it guilt, because you feel like you'd neglect them if you didn't? Shame? Fear of being alone? These are all very low vibrational emotions that won't serve you or them very much at all.

I'm not necessarily saying to cut them off; however, be very mindful and discerning with who you spend your precious time with. If they are people you can't just simply part ways with, such as family, make sure at least that the ratio of time that you are exposed to low vibes, limitation and negativity is by far outweighed by you exposing yourself to expansive people and inspirational input (for example via podcasts, audio books, live trainings, online group containers, workshops, events etc.), which are ultimately lifting you up.

#7 - Overwhelm
"There is way too much to do!" Being overwhelmed is a biggy, and it can freeze you on the spot if you're not careful.

The solution is to start with a strategic plan, outsource wherever you can, constantly prioritise and clear overwhelm and "having to be busy" programming. So many of us run the old thought program of having to work hard. However, it doesn't have to be this way! We all deserve ease and flow. Things can be easy, as long as we allow ourselves to believe it.

Flip the story by telling yourself, "I don't actually want to do all of this in one day. I'm choosing to focus on those steps that are of greatest priority right now and do them well".

You don't need to do everything at once. If you feel that this is you, focus on those steps that really get you further and do them now rather than getting lost in the length of your to-do list. Take focused and aligned action, rather than buying into overwhelm, which ultimately results in inaction!

If you're not even aware of what you're doing, and you are living within the victim mentality — aka "poor me" — then you won't even think that there is anything you can do to change your situation. You'll be thinking that everything is out of your control and that you're hard done by, as all those 'bad things' seem to only happen to you and not anyone else. You'll keep creating the same chains of events that you've always created and feel miserable.

If you're keen to take control back over your life — and instead of handing all your power away to all those 'bad things', 'bad people' and so on, and you are ready to take your power back over your own wellbeing, you could start with the following:

Ask yourself (after a big deep out-breath!):

- What's really important to you right now?
- What do you really want to achieve? Meaning, what rocks your boat and expands you?
- What feels super exciting to you?
- Then break it down: What does it take to get there?

Now is the time to get clear again about what it is that you really want to create or achieve. Make sure all your current projects are aligned with this outcome and that you're not getting distracted or side-tracked by any of them.

Once they are all aligned with your bigger vision, break them all down into little steps and keep chipping away at them. If you focus and keep reminding yourself what it is that you desire and why, and subsequently follow it through with action, then you'll be surprised how fast you'll get there.

Keep in mind that nothing that we do is an absolute must. There are always different options, we just need to come up with them and think of them. Usually this doesn't happen if we allow ourselves to get too stuck in our own head.

When we try to figure out everything in life with our head rather than our heart and intuition, our solutions will be limited to our mind and won't accurately reflect the possibilities out there. We'll be stuck in limitation, fear and scarcity — or at least limiting thinking — which are all not good places to be finding creative solutions from. We expect to find a solution to something with the same mind that has created the problem in the first place (or allowed it to happen) — which is kind of a paradox. And really, there are endless possibilities out there!

Therefore meditation, exercise and any other methods that help you get out of your head and into your body are a key part to creating a creative mindset.

Resistance can be (and usually is) a massive catalyst for growth!

If we persevere on our path and trust our inner voice and intuition despite the resistance, we are utilising the challenges we are facing as opportunities of growth. Resistance is an opportunity to grow in disguise! Resistance makes us look at stuff.

Key Takeaways:

- Resistance is a measure of the tendency to struggle against you moving forward. Our comfort zone, no matter if it's totally detrimental to our (mental) health and wellbeing or not, feels safe as it's known and familiar. Anything out of our comfort zone (i.e. our dreams and purpose) appears scary and threatening to our ego. Therefore, it pulls us back and keeps us small.

- There are 7 main Forms of Resistance to look out for that indicate that your comfort zone is being challenged: self-doubt, fear or lack of trust, distractions, denial, amnesia, aloneness and overwhelm.

- Get out of your head and into your body to tap into a creative mindset that allows for possibilities.

SPLIT-BRAIN HEMISPHERE SYNDROME

Something else to look out for is "Either-Or" or "Split Brain Hemisphere Syndrome". People often either struggle in the areas of love, health, fulfilment and / or money. They might find it easy to make lots of money but miss the fulfilment and positive impact that goes with it. Or they have put a lot of energy into making their life more fulfilling, slow and simple, or they simply find it is, but they've given up on the money part which ultimately means that they end up struggling to survive and pay their bills. Then there are others who are successful at making a positive impact with their work, but they are struggling with their health or relationships, or feel like they can only either be successful or a good mum/partner/friend etc, despite them knowing deep down that "having it all" is possible.

All of these scenarios are to a greater or lesser extent an expression of "Split Brain Hemisphere Syndrome", a term coined by Mission Mentor Nicola Grace.

Our brain hemispheres both govern a different aspect of our being. The right hemisphere governs the left half of our body and represents our creativity, flow, emotions, blissful states, love and connection; in short, our Yin energy.

The left brain hemisphere governs the right side of our body and represents our structural, mathematical and systematic approach; in other words our Yang energy. Most of us have the tendency to lean towards either one of these energies and aspects of our being more than the other. Therefore, we tend to be either more creative or more structural in our approach to life. Again, we all have both aspects within us — none can go without the other — so it's good to balance out our approach and "marry our brain halves".

The integrated Brain
= Both Brain Hemispheres Working Well Together

Left Brain Hemisphere
- responsible for controlling the right side of the body
- performs tasks that have to do with logic, strategy and a sense of order and time, such as in science and mathematics
- Yang Energy (masculine)
- key areas of life: WORK, the CORPORATE World, CONSISTENCY, STRATEGY

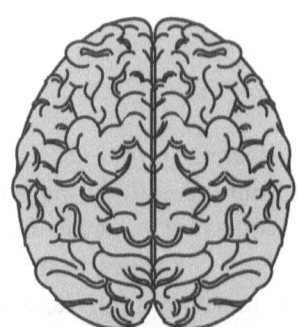

Right Brain Hemisphere
- coordinates the left side of the body
- performs tasks that have do with creativity, intuition, the arts and flow (not linear)
- Yin Energy (feminine)
- key areas of life: PURPOSE, LOVE, CONNECTION, FUN, BLISS, SPIRIT, FLOW

Generally, we have "Split Brain Hemishere Syndrome"
EITHER purpose OR day job
EITHER love & connection OR money
EITHER flow OR strategy
EITHER fun OR consistency
EITHER family OR success

...Unless we work on ourself and "marry" our brain halves.

Clearing lifetimes worth of emotional baggage, conditioning and upper limits >>> an integrated brain that allows you to "have it all"

© Sand Mew

With "Split Brain Hemisphere Syndrome", people see themselves EITHER making good money / being a great business owner / being successful OR living their purpose / being a connected parent, etc.

It all goes back to the old days, when people used to EITHER be royal and wealthy OR hard working in the fields. Or they were EITHER spiritual and healers who got looked after by others OR working. In various places of the world this role distribution is still being carried out today: In India, for example, there are many Saddhus who live in the mountains. They're called "the enlightened", smoke chillums all day, talk about philosophy and relax, whilst the others work and bring them food. The roles are clear, and no one would question their place.

In the West, however, we mostly don't live with this setup anymore. Most of us have to look after our own food, no matter what jobs we have. We all have bills, washing, and earthly matters to take care of — no matter if we help others with their spiritual and health needs, are a philosopher, meditate or not.

As our thinking is still heavily governed by the generations that came before us, as mentioned in previous chapters, we haven't yet completely let go of this old paradigm in which healers and saints look after the spiritual and health needs of their community and in turn get looked after with food and shelter.

This conditioning of our thinking has been contributing to the difficulty that most people have in imagining that they could really make a living or good income from healing, transforming, acting, serving or expressing themselves in a way that's deeply meaningful to them.

The same goes for being an amazing parent AND successful business owner. If we haven't seen certain concepts being lived well together, or hold an old charge that keeps our brain hemispheres split, we'll have a very hard time even imagining both of them being possible at once. Most of the time, we'll feel like we have to choose one of the two concepts and in the meantime turn our back towards the other - which in most cases will create inner turmoil and friction.

However, we *can* have both (whatever it is). All it takes is for us to bring our brain halves and thinking together. We don't need to fit into this old paradigm of "either or" anymore. We can choose to live our passions, spirituality, help others, be wealthy and amazing parents or partners - all at the same time.

We need to release all the conditioning, beliefs, patterns and traumas that keep our brain hemispheres separate, so that they can unite and work smoothly together. This may include rewiring our money mindset, away from employee thinking to the one of an entrepreneur. However, it may also involve shifting our inner perspectives and programming around how we perceive the world, being parents or lovers, etc.

Doing this work is truly life changing and I love seeing the results my clients get with this on the daily!

Key Takeaways:

- People often either struggle in the areas of love, health, fulfilment and/ or money. This is referred to as "Either-Or" or "Split Brain Hemisphere Syndrome".

- Our left (L) versus our right (R) brain hemisphere both governs a different aspect of our being: Our Yang, masculine, structured aspects and right side of our body (L) and our Yin, feminine, creative and flowing aspects, as well as left side of our body (R).

- In order to "have it all" or allow ourselves to be able to see and create both those aspects, we need to integrate and "marry" our brain hemispheres, which we can do through clearing work.

UPPER LIMITS AND EXTERNAL LIMITERS

Last but not least, there are upper limits to acknowledge. On the journey of expansion, especially if we keep up-levelling from one stage of entrepreneurial wealth and freedom creation to the next, we'll keep facing and hitting upper limits of how much peace, joy, excitement, money, followers, views, revenue, profits etc we can allow ourselves to receive or experience before we subconsciously sabotage it.

The great thing is, with the tools of *The Spiral* by Dane Tomas and *Take The Brakes Off™ - Self Clearing Method*, we can simply "clear up" the percentage of how much we allow ourselves to receive / experience and open up the "gates" so to speak for way more to come through!

Now, and this is something I had suspected for quite some time and was confirmed by a spiritual business mentor I had worked with in 2016; there are energetic domes that have been placed over all our continents. They come at different heights and form upper limits for us. If we're not aware of them, they simply keep us from fully tapping into our limitlessness and from shining. So they keep us stumped in our growth, much like weeds under shade-cloths. Every continent has a different height of their dome. It's linked with the well-known tall poppy syndrome, that's very active in Australia. In America it's definitely higher. In a lot of places in Europe it's even lower.

We can't remove or clear away these domes, as that would be violating Lore and would entrap us. However, we can remove the charge, emotions, interferences, entities and any other links that we hold in our body by clearing them, which in turn means we can grow and expand beyond them without hindrance.

I refer to them as external limiters. Just as much as it's imperative to know about internal upper limits, such as having a limit around how much you're allowing yourself to be visible, it's also imperative to know about external upper limits. If unnoticed, they will act out as sabotage that keeps you energetically small and not fully playing out. They have to be dealt with, so you can expand and live your limitless potential, and fully shine and be free.

We need to work through and acknowledge what needs to be acknowledged, and pin to the wall what's external and simply in the way to hold us back from expressing our limitless version. When we do this, we usually get rewarded with a big growth spurt or a breakthrough of some sort, as we've grown and expanded our comfort zone and/or popped through the other side of external limiters - which is ultimately what we are here for.

I myself had lots of self-doubt over the years, especially when I started working on becoming more visible with my message, which was strange for me in the beginning as I had always been a pretty self-confident person. However, working on my purpose, making the decision to bring my whole life into 100% alignment (and not just 98%) after selling our franchise shop in 2014 and then saying yes to my dreams and unapologetically sharing my message with the world, brought my biggest resistance patterns to the surface. I gave them no chance to hide anymore, as I was determined to grow. I still am and always will be.

We are spirits having a human experience. We are meant to expand and grow, despite all our programming to stay small.

If you keep looking at yourself, paying attention to your patterns of resistance and working on your inner connection and alignment, you're on the sure-fire path to breaking through your limitations and becoming unstoppable. And that's my wish for you and the world!

If what we are experiencing is inflicted on us by an externally created entity or interference, or collective sabotage pattern of keeping us small, we need to clear it and what's active within us that allows it to be there. It takes a high level of discernment and understanding of what's ultimately benevolent and what isn't. (We can also make it super simple by muscle testing.)

Doing so will allow us to free ourselves, move past collective upper limits and release their grip on us. In order to safely do so, it's highly important to follow specific steps and guidelines. All my clients benefit from this and I teach these in my *Take The Brakes Off™ - Self-Clearing* course and *Self Clearing Leaders Program* too.

Key Takeaways:

- On the journey of expansion, especially if we keep up-levelling from one stage of entrepreneurial wealth and freedom creation to the next, we'll keep facing and hitting upper limits of how much peace, joy, excitement, money, followers, views, revenue, profits etc we can allow ourselves to receive or experience before we subconsciously sabotage it.

- There are energetic domes that have been placed over all our continents. They come at different heights and form upper limits for humanity. If we're not aware of them, they simply keep us from fully tapping into our limitlessness.

- We are spirits having a human experience. We are meant to expand and grow, despite all our programming to stay small.

GETTING UNSTUCK WHEN THINGS DON'T FLOW

If you're feeling like things aren't flowing all that well and you're more pushing against things, then stop for a moment. Believe me, this is such an overlooked but pivotal part of this whole process! It's all about continuously coming back to your centre and realigning.

Ask yourself the following questions:

- Am I still in alignment with my big vision?
- Am I trying too hard and am I stifling the outcomes during the process as a result?
- Have I lost sight of my own truth, values or expression modalities?
- Am I chasing someone else's values and ideals?
- Is a sabotage pattern (internally or externally created) playing out?
- Am I focusing too much on lack or the past, instead of where I want to go and feeling into being there already?

No matter what, if things don't flow, take a step back and reassess. Make sure you realign with your dream vision and values and keep letting go of anything that's no longer in alignment.

You'll need to be a vibrational match to what you desire, so if you're feeling all stuck and limited, it's not going to attract what you want.

No matter how much you sleep, or how much movement, journaling and setting goals you do, if your attitude and mindset keep you stuck in limitation, lack, fear, blame and stress, then you need to change this. Watch your thoughts by being super aware of where they are going. Write them down if need be, otherwise simply sit and listen whilst doing the dishes, driving, walking, jogging etc.

Don't mix being a vibrational match up with being "over the top positive". You won't do yourself a favour if you try to suppress your negative self-talk and feelings, and instead focus on being overly positive alone. I know that this is contradicting the teachings of so many coaches out there, that tell you to do everything in your power to avoid having even just one single negative thought!

I've been finding that if the positive statement or affirmation is just not your truth at that very moment, then take a moment to give this negative self-talk a voice, so it feels heard and can let go.

In order to give this negative self-talk a chance to get acknowledged, write down what it says as a sign to your subconscious that now that the comments, thoughts and beliefs are written down, your subconscious doesn't have to keep remembering them and keep reminding you of them.

Most importantly, really acknowledge all that's coming up for you, and ask yourself what it is that the various emotions you are experiencing are trying to tell you;

- Is there frustration coming up that's trying to show you that you are living out of alignment in one or several areas of your life?
- Is anxiety pulling on you, as a suppressed fear of shining your light too brightly and bringing up "Tall Poppy Syndrome"? Or is it pulling on you, because you are trying to live someone else's values, resulting in you losing your own centre?
- Is depression showing up to show you that you're exhausted and can't see a way out?
- Is jealousy nudging you in the direction of where you actually want to be in your life?
- Are you having a niggling truth coming up that you're too scared to listen to, as it would mean big changes in your life that you're not prepared to face?

Really acknowledge all parts of yourself and your reality. Instead of suppressing them or letting yourself get carried away by them, take all your feelings into account. Let them show you what they are ACTUALLY trying to signal to you and allow yourself to follow their guidance. If you do so, you'll

129

find it way easier to truly move on and to start FEELING positive about life and yourself again — authentically and deeply, with clarity.

Once you've acknowledged where you're at and possibly why, it's time to take the breaks off again. Get clear about your limiting belief systems and sabotage patterns around your next steps, clear yourself and lock in new beliefs and patterns. Clear the charge around the emotions and beliefs that are triggering you and then reframe them. This step might require some deep clearing/ healing sessions and support, but they will do wonders.

This part of the process can be the hardest of them all. You need to continuously check in with yourself: Are you actually allowing yourself to be all of you and have those dreams of yours? What's the hidden payoff for not being there yet? What part of you feels safer to still be stuck in the known, unwanted limitation? What fears do you have around getting there?

Also become aware of how you are talking to yourself. Would you talk like this to a good friend?

It's common to beat oneself up if things don't seem "good enough" or your progress "far enough" yet. However, it's really important to stop this approach, as soon as you become aware of it, because it achieves only the opposite; it paralyses you.

I like to refer to the analogy of a flower:

Imagine a beautiful sunflower in front of you. What happens if you stomp it?

Exactly, it gets mushed to the ground.

Similarly, what we do in our internal dialogue is pretty much like stomping on a sunflower and then saying to it "Why aren't you bigger, taller, brighter and shinier?"

Whenever I see this picture with my inner eye, I have to laugh. Can you see just how ridiculous we can be to ourselves?

What we need to do instead is get off our flower and let it BE. It knows how to grow very well. As long as we provide it with water, sun, soil and a bit of space, it's very happy. All that we achieve by wanting to control the flower's outcomes is that we get into the way of its natural ability to grow and shine and turn its head towards the sun.

However, if we can get out of the way, and let it do its thing, it'll know what to do. We simply need to hold space for it and look after its basic needs. Those needs are our 3-5 top values; again, you can find them out by doing Dr Demartini's free Value Test online. That way it can be, do and have whatever it needs to. That's all!

So instead of beating yourself up about not being "there" yet, why not focus on the actual progress you have made since overcoming the worst stage/ the beginning of your journey, even if there seems to be little to show for it so far. It's unbelievable what a bit of gratitude to self and a healthy sense of pride can do for one's progress! It'll speed things up immensely, I promise.

Keep in mind, there'll be ups, when you'll have lots of energy and feel high with inspiration, but they'll also be followed with lows. Triggers can come up. You are a multidimensional being on a journey of growing and expanding into a more and more authentically expressed version of yourself.

There is no such thing as a perfect life and happy ending. We are never completely "there." We'll always experience the ups and downs of life, the messy days and will get challenged — especially just before having the next breakthrough on our journey of expansion. But we can get to a place where we're able to navigate these problems faster, smoother and in a more empowered way than ever before.

Because we have a safe place of inner certainty to come back to, even if there is a storm coming past on the outside.

Furthermore, if we don't resist the emotions and struggles that are part of life but instead take them as signposts to show us the way back "home" to our inner centre, then we understand the deeper meaning of everything and can navigate life in a way that allows us to feel deeply connected, fulfilled, joyful, at peace and thriving – no matter what's happening on the outside.

So, in a nutshell, the essential secret of success is: Know what you really desire deep in your core and why, plus make sure that no subconscious beliefs and/or traumas are telling your being that you wouldn't be safe if you got there. Then keep taking inspired action towards it.

Key Takeaways:

- If things don't flow, take a step back and reassess. Make sure you realign with your dream vision and values and keep letting go of anything that's no longer in alignment.

- You'll need to be a vibrational match to what you desire, so if you're feeling all stuck and limited, it's not going to attract what you want. You need to up your vibe.

- Don't mix being a vibrational match up with being "over the top positive". By-passing won't work, as it's inauthentic and the universe will know. You need to fully acknowledge anything that comes up.

- Continuously check in with yourself: Are you actually allowing yourself to be all of you and have those dreams of yours? What's the hidden payoff for not being there yet?

WHAT DOES 'CLEARING' MEAN + WHY WOULD WE WANT TO DO IT?

Now what does clearing actually mean? It doesn't mean cutting the emotion off or ignoring it, even though the name might imply this. It's actually quite the opposite. Clearing does not mean ignoring it or pretending it's not there. Clearing also doesn't mean reiki or other energy healing methods.

I'm not saying that they're not effective, however, they don't work the same way, as they don't necessarily acknowledge the root cause or what your potential via your body is trying to tell you. If we really, truly want to take the brakes off and clear our baggage, and really free ourselves deeply at the core of our being, we need to ...

1. Dive deep and find out first what's really going on in our subconscious (via kinesiology, finger-testing, holding strong intentions and frames in our mind and potentially utilising the Emotion Chart).
2. Clear anything external (i.e., Interdimensionals, contracts and agreements) out of the way first, then feel into those underlying trapped emotions and acknowledge them.
3. Clear and neutralise the charge around the sensations we feel.

By utilising Kinesiology, finger testing, strong intentions and frames in our mind and potentially utilising the Emotion Chart, we sometimes uncover things that we would have never thought of before. Our mind doesn't always tell us what's going on. For example, you might feel tired and flat, but what's really going on is that you got triggered by a phone call that happened two hours ago and now trapped emotions such as Frustration, Helplessness and Lack of Trust are active.

There might also be external upper limits, entities or interferences in the way that are blocking us from being 100% in our body.

After clearing anything external out of the way first, we need to feel into where in our body we can sense them, how they feel and how they affect us in our body and life. We also need to allow ourselves to go deep and acknowledge what they are trying to do FOR us.

Very often we feel powerlessness towards the world and things we feel we can't influence. We can feel limited or scared. We can feel completely out of control in regard to certain situations. However, if we go deeply inwards, and really acknowledge what's hiding in our subconscious as well as mind and body, we can remember who we are and truly free ourselves. We can neutralise the charge that we are feeling towards different sensations, situations, people and dynamics, and therefore take the trigger, stress, pain, tension or sensation out of it.

And that's what the clearing refers to. We are clearing the charge. We take the power out of the charge. And therefore, re-empowering ourselves with what it's actually trying to do for us.

The more we can neutralise and take the charge out of something, i.e. the anger, frustration, helplessness, powerlessness, etc that we may feel towards a situation, the more we can take our power back and realise that we create the outcome. The more we can come back to our centre, shift internally and clear the charge, the more free we become.

And that's what we need to do so we can truly lead with authenticity, create our desires, live our dreams and live the big visions that we have.

Taking The Brakes Off means you can be ...

- Fully present in your life without putting yourself down and being distracted
- Relaxed and joyous in your being in any given moment in time, instead of having stories of shame, fear, doubts or worries and what people might be thinking filling your mind
- Free of all that and be 100% present and therefore live your purpose and potential

Taking The Brakes Off means ...

- Freeing yourself of old baggage by fully facing the dark parts, shadow and traits that you hate or have an aversion to, the stuff you feel the most. By truly facing those really icky, dark and sticky situations, and fully owning them back, you take your power back into your own hands.

- You set yourself free and that in turn means your heart is open. You can feel deeply without taking stuff on.
- You can get into flow, you can manifest at ease and create an amazing life and impact.

When you clear your baggage, when you take the breaks off, the result will be:

- Certainty
- A deep remembering of who you really are
- Inner peace, calm and harmony
- Joy
- A deep sense of trust that you've got this and will be supported
- No more anxiety, no more doubt, no more hesitance
- True empowerment

And what does that mean in tangible terms?

- Knowing your direction with clarity and focus
- Being productive
- Having more harmonious and deeply connected relationships
- Feeling loved and seen for who you are
- Being authentic on stage/in front of others, being seen and received for your message in the world
- Receiving support and love, i.e. being able to hire an A-team that's value aligned, fully has got your back and that can run your business or that you can lead it with
- Turning into a magnet in your business and life
- Unapologetically being you and expressing yourself authentically on all levels, creating your dreams - again on all levels.

You see, the list is endless really.

Key Takeaways:

'Clearing' doesn't mean cutting the emotion off or ignoring it. Instead, we can neutralise the charge that we are feeling towards different sensations, situations, people and dynamics, and therefore take the trigger, stress, pain, tension or sensation out of it.

The more we can neutralise and take the charge out of something; i.e. the anger, frustration, helplessness, powerlessness, etc that we may feel towards a situation, the more we can take our power back and create the outcome that we desire.

Taking The Brakes Off means freeing yourself of old baggage, setting yourself free and getting into flow, so you can manifest at ease and create an amazing life and impact.

11 SIGNS THAT YOU'RE READY TO TAKE THE BRAKES OFF™

Generally, you'll know when you have the brakes on. You won't feel satisfied with where things are at and/or you simply don't feel good.

My clients describe this frustration a lot when they contact me for the first time to work with me (no matter in what "category" of life); they feel like they're sabotaging or something is holding them back, and they can't tell what it is. It's like their mind and their body believe different things, and this incongruence creates a vibrational mismatch that manifests in them having to either work way too hard for their desired results, or not receiving the outcomes they're yearning for altogether (cognitive dissonance); either professionally or personally - or both.

They might have anxiety, self doubt, frequent bouts of frustration or feel blocked.

Or they generally feel 'fine', with finances, business and relationships going well, but certainly don't feel like they're living their potential.

Following are a few signs to assist you in identifying whether you've got the brakes on, and therefore trapped emotions, conditioning, upper limits and interferences in the way:

1. **You're playing small.**
   If you've got trapped emotions, conditioning, upper limits and so on ruling the show, chances are you'll feel like hiding and dimming your light.

2. **You have anxiety in times of upleveling or expansion.**
   But also at other times. You feel anxiety, stress, restlessness. You overthink.

3. **You feel tired, exhausted and drained.**
   No wonder! You're trying to exhilarate with the hand brakes on! This is not only going to lead to a worn out vehicle (your body), but it will also lead you to procrastination and sabotage.

4. **You're spinning your wheels, feel paralyzed or that you're sabotaging.**
   You know what you need to do, but you just can't seem to do it. This is a clear sign that you need to start self clearing or get support right now.

5. **You feel unproductive and find it difficult to focus.**
   Trapped emotions, conditioning, interferences, Interdimensionals, whatever is going on, will make it very difficult for you to stay productive and focused. So if you're keen to get stuff done and you wonder what is going on and holding you back, there is a reason.. These patterns will hold you back unless you address them.

6. **Things feel hard.**
   I've said this already in the last five points, but just one more time. Having the brakes on will make everything extremely hard for you. You won't be productive, feel focused, or like you can do stuff. You might not even believe in yourself anymore.

7. **You risk relationships, money and other things that are important for you in your life.**
   You might be argumentative and jeopardise your relationship(s), for example, close down a business or make some other major life changes, such as or breaking up from your partner or business partner.

8. **You've got brain fog or feel blocked and that things are too hard.**
   You feel you're not good enough. You doubt and hesitate.

9. **You feel you've got no time for this or are too busy for change.**
   You've got stuff going on. You can't afford it. You can't do it. You don't have the time, space, money, or any resources to do that. Well, that's the very reason why you need to do the work in the first place.

10. **Things are breaking or going wrong.**
    Stuff may be happening, seemingly out of your control; for example one of your work vehicles breaking down, followed by another accident, followed by some other errors. Another example is that your email or payment channels aren't working well, as if something is blocking them. Chances are, there is!

11. **Living a reality that is not matching your big dreams.**
    You won't feel as expanded, great, excited or ignited as you would if you'd be fully in flow and alignment with yourself.

Having the brakes on; meaning having trapped emotions, conditioning, upper limits and so on ruling the show, will create havoc in your life and in your relationships. It can lead to major losses - monetary and emotionally.

So it's really, really important to address whatever is going on, because you can make big mistakes if you ignore them.

However, once you deal with what's going on and clear it, things stop breaking and happening. You feel your heart open again. You start feeling fully connected again, with yourself and others. You can completely repair your business(es), relationships and any situations, if they're aligned, once you've dealt with your stuff.

Whatever is going on that shows you you've got the brakes on, the rule of thumb is:

If you're ...

- Frustrated about where you're currently at
- Sick of what you're currently experiencing
- Drawn to what you've learnt in this book
- Simply clear on the fact that you're ready to ignite your potential

... you're ready to take the brakes off!

Key Takeaways:

- Having the brakes on; meaning having trapped emotions, conditioning, upper limits and so on ruling the show, will create havoc in your life and in your relationships. It can lead to major losses — monetarily and emotionally.

- Taking the brakes off will lead to inner certainty, a deep remembering of who you really are, inner peace, calm and harmony, joy, a deep sense of trust that you've got this and will be supported, no more doubt and hesitance, but true empowerment.

- If you're frustrated about where you're at and ready for things to be different, you're ready to take the brakes off.

CONCLUSION

Congrats, you made it to the end of the book! Well done for diving deep into all the things that hold us back and put hand brakes onto our potential.

To recap, in order to ignite your potential and have it all — fulfilment, love, money, inspiration, energy and making a positive impact — you'll be required to do the inner work of clearing out old baggage and conditioning which is limiting you from moving forward and even seeing what's possible in the first place. Without stepping into a new identity first, that lives the next level in your business and life that you're envisioning, you won't be able to create it — or at least not without a lot of sacrifice.

In order to step into this new identity, you'll need to let go of whatever it is that's keeping the handbrakes on; you'll need to excavate the 'gold nuggets' of wisdom these hand brakes have been holding for you - often for a very long time.

You'll need to clear the trauma and conditioning that is locked into our DNA, physical body and subconscious, all of which are holding you back in the "safe" comfort zone. That way you'll be able to continuously expand your comfort zone, as is required when you step into more visibility, income and impact.

And why is this important to more people than just yourself, you might ask?

Because we as people, as humanity, can go for our desires and really shift the state of the world by doing so. This realisation alone is life changing. Every single individual's awakening to this understanding is pivotal and contributes in a way bigger sense than what is perceivable at first sight.

As I have mentioned several times throughout the book, every individual counts. Because we are all interconnected; any individual's increase in consciousness also raises to some degree the consciousness of everyone on the planet. Remember, according to Dr David Hawkins, although only 15% of the world's population is above the critical consciousness level of 200, the collective power of that 15% has the weight to counterbalance the negativity of the remaining 85%.

By doing 'the work' and focusing on your own evolution, you're already making a positive impact on many others by the positive ripple it creates, even without physically being in contact with them. The more you expand your direct impact with the work or things you do in your community or the world, this impact gets even bigger.

That's why I love what I do so much. Every single individual that gets ignited will create positive ripples. We all have the opportunity to raise our level of awareness, if we are ready to do so. Once we follow the inner calling to step up, explore, heal, release, learn and expand, there is no going back. The more we *systematically* clear our baggage, with the aim to free ourselves from trauma, shame, dogma etc and to connect with our desires and dreams, and take action, the more we raise our frequency and consciousness level. This will not only impact the way we see ourselves and the world, and up-level what we attract, but also our thoughts, perspective and approach. Our entire mindset will shift without us having to change each thought at a time. We step into a new identity with so much more ease.

Sooner rather than later we will find ourselves on the quest to find our purpose, and if we are determined enough, we can really start making a difference in the world by fully expressing who we are and the authentic truth we have to share.

We all have so many gifts, strengths and stories to share and our message counts, so we need to get out there and do what we're here for. No matter if your purpose and big why is based on the environment, providing sustainable building solutions, or whether that's coaching, teaching, consulting and unlocking people, or whether it's about building big businesses that offer workplaces and a beautiful environment for others to learn, share and grow. It doesn't really matter what your purpose is, it matters to the people that you need to impact. Therefore, we need to make sure that every single one of us gets unlocked so we can do what we're here for and bring the puzzle piece that we need to bring to the big picture that we're all part of.

I'd love to empower you with tools, frameworks and your own intuition, so you can deepen your connection with it and live from that place, and so you can understand what your body is trying to tell you. That way, you can really reconnect with your unique limitless potential and lead from that place. Again, it's all about living authentically from the heart, being open, receptive and accepting, whilst honouring your own truth. That way, you can live your purpose, create your dreams and make the biggest impact possible.

With the tools, methods, frameworks and maps I use and teach in my journeys and programs, we level up to higher levels of consciousness really fast. Now you have the opportunity to learn how to do so for yourself, by learning the *Take the Brakes Off*™ *Self Clearing Method*.

So, I ask you one more time:

What will change for you when you live your true potential and take your life, business, relationships and impact to the next level?

The time is now.

Together we rise.

NEXT STEPS
TAKE THE BRAKES OFF™ SELF CLEARING ECOURSE

(The Foundations)

Learn the foundations of self-clearing
so you can ignite your potential + create the life of your wildest dreams!

Are you a business owner, achiever, visionary, driven individual who's receptive and feels a lot?

Chances are that you've been feeling overwhelmed at times, swamped by peoples' 'stuff' or just ready for the next level of purpose, impact, authentic visibility and wealth - but stuff seems to be in the way.

Let me introduce you to THE most self-empowering Self-Clearing course that's going to change your life, business, relationships AND goal creation forever:

Take The Brakes Off™ Self-Clearing Method

An 8 Module (33+ Lessons) online Course with high-level, first class support from Sand Mew (Holistic Business and Transformation Mentor with 20 years practitioner experience) and her team.

What you'll learn:

- **Tools and strategic road maps to clear your baggage**, triggers, conditioning and upper limits - Fast, powerfully and effectively (meaning, how you can change feeling stress, anxiety, a weird off feeling, anger, frustration ..you name it.. into neutrality in a matter of a few seconds or minutes)

- **How to hold your Space as an empath** or energetically highly aware person (say bye to brain fog and feeling wiped out after seeing people or being in crowds and feel clear and energised instead!)

- **How to free yourself** of brain fog, overwhelm, head spins, etc. and tap into productivity, focus and flow instead.

- **How to improve your relationships** and create harmony within yourself and your relationships within seconds or minutes.

- **How to get out of our own way, kick self sabotage in the butt** and move forward with more clarity and confidence.

- **Tools and strategic roadmaps to clarifying your aligned goals**, removing any seen or unseen obstacles out of the way and creating your goals in 3D reality.

- **Tools to tap into flow** and become unstoppable.

And much more!

*"**A very useful and practical skills course** that can be used by anyone in any situation. It should be taught to everyone!"*
— Naomi, Business Owner

*"**I love the easiness of it all, the quick release and so many different aspects in life we can apply it on.** I would love to see everybody learning and applying this powerful modality. It then can change the world, I'm sure."*
— Ben, Business Owner

"I'm learning a powerful tool to confirm my intuition and clear triggers, and claim my space.
I really like the examples and explanations of practical examples. I really appreciated your calm and centred approach and grounded responses to the group."

— Anna, Online Marketer and Investor

"Sand is a wealth of knowledge and delivers information with clarity, humour and passion! Would definitely do more programs, I'm keen to learn more!!"

— Bonnie, Therapist

"It's great finding a technique to help with not only my own self improvement but also others'. I've been learning self clearing techniques to help me reach my full potential.
I love Sand's style of teaching and the visualisation. There is so much to learn here, it's so exciting!
This self clearing technique is a god-send for me to get out of my head and limiting beliefs and step into my purpose."

— Dimity, Blogger

"Sand is a delightful and insightful presenter. She has an amazing amount of knowledge which she shares in an enjoyable and thought provoking way."
— Kevin Blair, General Manager

"This course has been giving me empowering information to use with myself, my family and all or any that come into my life. The delivery of all the information was really great! What an amazing facilitator!
Thank you for shining your light, Sand, and empowering others to do the same."
— Jandamarra, Artist and Thought Leader

To find out more, visit:

https://programs.sandmew.com/ttbo-self-clearing

THE ULTIMATE BREAKTHROUGH JOURNEY / THE SPIRAL

Free yourself of the largest amount of emotional baggage, trauma, conditioning and upper limits in the shortest amount of time, so you can remember who you are and increase your sense of flow, purpose, wealth and impact with inner certainty.

You've got a big vision. You are a Conscious leader, impact-driven entrepreneur or business owner, who is ready for the next level.

However, you've been hitting some road blocks. Sabotage, self doubt, imposter or tall poppy syndrome, overwhelm, anxiety, spinning your wheels, getting triggered, loss of mojo .. or simply like things could be even better than they already are.

Join Sand for her 8-week signature program (via 1:1 or intimate group journey of 4 participants max, with additional support) available from anywhere in the World via Zoom. As an Advanced Spiral Practitioner who's facilitated more than 250 journeys and tens of thousands of clearings so far, let Sand guide you.

Up your level of consciousness, take the brakes off and change your paradigm.

What you'll *find* is:

- Deep Inner Certainty, Calm + Peace
- Confidence + Inner Strength
- Authentic Leadership + improved Relationships
- Increased Resilience
- Clarity, Direction + Flow
- Manifesting the Results you Desire with Ease

"I highly recommend Sand Mew and her work.
The shifts I've had were crazy. *I love the clearing and the healing process and the whole journey. Words can't explain how good it is."*

— Kamal T., Business Owner

"I am having people in my life tell me, "I feel like you're finally showing up as you"
My relationship with myself has shifted. I've gained a deep level of certainty and trust in self and a stronger connection to my awareness. I have become even clearer on my vision and stepped even more into leadership. My purpose is clearer than ever. I let go of any work and services that do not align with who I really am and it feels easy. Opportunities have opened up.
Sand sees YOU.
She sees past the chaos and has the ability to see the true essence of who you really are and also a sense of what you are here for. I feel this deeply.
She has the ability to call you out and bring you back to presence whilst also being incredibly nurturing. If you are thinking about working with Sand, Do it. You will never EVER regret it.

— Paula Bailey, Leadership Consultant

"I've nicknamed Sand 'my Secret Weapon'"

— Sean Soole, Business Mentor + Educator

Find out more:
https://www.sandmew.com/

Check out tons of testimonials here (written and videos):
https://www.sandmew.com/testimonials

CONNECT WITH SAND MEW

Thank you so much for coming on this journey with me! I hope you've gained insight, inspiration and clarity around your next steps by reading this book.

As a brand, it's our purpose to ignite, inspire and empower limitless potential in conscious leaders around the world.

It's our mission to spark deep transformation within leaders throughout the world, so they are empowered to live their purpose and enjoy amazingly abundant and fulfilling lives.

I'm deeply and passionately dedicated to this work and envision a global movement of conscious and self clearing leaders who move beyond their limits and create greater positive impact.

If you have a friend, family member, colleague or team member that you think would benefit from this book, please share, pass it around, buy the book as gifts and recommend it to your local library, so that this message can touch those who need it the most!

This is how you can find us and connect online:

Website: https://www.sandmew.com/

Facebook: www.facebook.com/sandmewmentoringclearing

Instagram: https://www.instagram.com/sand_mew/

LinkedIn: http://linkedin.com/in/sand-mew-0a46939a

YouTube: https://www.youtube.com/@sandmew

Email Sand directly: sand@sandmew.com

If you'd like to have me speak at an event or book me for your next corporate workshop for your leadership teams or programs, please email me at sand@sandmew.com or visit https://www.sandmew.com/speaking

And if you're ready to take the brakes off and free yourself of lifetimes worth of emotional baggage, conditioning and upper limits in the shortest amount of time, book a complimentary 30min chat with us now: https:// www.sandmew.com/

ACKNOWLEDGEMENTS

Finally, I'd like to extend many thanks to a number of people who have been there for me and supported me and my journey, my work and our mission.

Dave Thompson and the team at Inspirational Book Writers (IBW) for holding an exceptional and powerful container of coaching and mentorship to allow me to write the bulk of my book at the online book writing intensive. Thank you for all you guys do from the start of 'conception' of an idea until the launch. You make the book writing, *Publish + Launch* journey smooth and you're a joy to work with!

My husband Jonny Mew for being on this journey with me, doing the work and believing in me. Thank you for being there for our beautiful boys whenever I've been in creative hibernation mode to get my work out into the world and supporting me with powerful clears whenever needed throughout the years.

Arlo and Bodhi for being the most compassionate, understanding and supportive young boys, whilst knowing what you want and need. Keep going for your dreams! I am so grateful to be able to call myself your mum.

My parents, my sister Sylvia and brother Jochen in Germany for their love and support right from the start. Mum especially, thank you for teaching me what it means to love unconditionally. I'm forever grateful. Thank you for teaching me to believe in my dreams, to always follow my heart and never give up. Thank you for trusting me from a tiny age.

"Opa" Manz for the profound wisdom you imparted to me as a girl. You taught me what true leadership means.

Sean Soole and the Inner Circle team, Dave Thompson, Jen Jeavons and the team at Pixel Palace, Karla Pizzica, Daniel Kress and specific friends and clients (you know who you are) who all contributed key business and brand strategies and supported me in getting my inner game on point.

Dane Tomas, for creating the amazing modality called The Spiral which has given me a systematic framework to pour all my modalities, skills, knowledge and knowing into.

Dr Demartini, Dr Joe Dispenza, Roger Hamilton, Kel Davis, Amanda Frances, Katrina Ruth, Denise Duffield-Thomas, Marie Forleo, Nicola Grace and the many many influencers, healers, teachers, ancient guides and wise ones whose names might never be known in the Western World but will forever be edged into my cells, that I've had the privilege to learn from all over the world for the past few decades.

My team member Jen— Thanks for being an amazing integrator and supporting me in bringing my visions to life!

And last but not least, my many students and clients who teach me so much and encourage me to put my ideas onto paper— without you, this book and my previous one would not be here today!

ABOUT THE AUTHOR

Sand Mew is an igniter. A holistic business mentor, international bestselling author, speaker, entrepreneur and global educator in transformation.

Sand has been fascinated by reading bodies and feet from a very young age onwards. Facing and overcoming a severe sickness with 16, enabled her to gain an even deeper understanding of the interconnectedness of body, mind and spirit.

After more than two decades of study, travelling the world, many qualifications, 20 years of practice, creating her own accredited modality called *The Footprint Connection*™ (connecting people with their unique footprint on planet earth), facilitating more than 250 *The Ultimate Breakthrough Journeys* (Sand's version of *The Spiral*) plus tens of thousands of clearings with clients and working with visionary leaders from all over the world for many years, Sand has synthesised all that she knows to offer powerful and transformative experiences to leaders of every kind.

Moreover, Sand has run, managed and owned multiple businesses. Sand is a serial entrepreneur and investor. This unique fusion of abilities, skills and experience has not only supported Sand's clients to more flow, purpose, success, wealth and impact, but also herself to build multi 6-figure purpose-led businesses impacting conscious leaders around the globe.

Sand lives at the Sunshine Coast of Australia, where she loves spending quality time with her husband and their two beautiful boys. Apart from loving her deep client work and creating powerful transformational experiences, she loves going to the lookout, travelling and dancing.

As a practitioner, Sand helps conscious leaders, visionaries and business owners move beyond the limitations they carry consciously and subconsciously, using a systematic approach to overcome their greatest challenges and create the life of their wildest dreams.

Notes

Notes.

Notes

Notes

Notes

www.ingramcontent.com/pod-product-compliance
Lightning Source LLC
Chambersburg PA
CBHW030447290526
45786CB00001B/476